Curriculum-Based Therapy Activities
Volume II

Growing Things
Cosas que crecen

Food
La comida

Weather
El clima

Places We Go
Lugares donde vamos

Transportation
El transporte

Insects
Los insectos

English and Spanish Edition

Bilinguistics, Inc.

www.bilinguistics.com

Copyright © 2016 Bilinguistics, Inc.
All rights reserved. Printed in the U.S.A.

Published by Bilinguistics, Inc.

1505 Koenig Lane, Austin, TX 78756

For more information, contact Bilinguistics, Inc. or visit us at: www.bilinguistics.com.

Permission is granted for the user to print the material contained in this publication in limited form for individual use only. Copies of this material may not be reproduced for entire agencies, used for commercial sale, stored in a retrieval system, or transmitted in any form (electronically, recording, mechanically, web, etc.) without the publisher's explicit permission.

ISBN-13: 978-1514895139

ISBN-10: 1514895137

INTRODUCTION

As a young speech pathologist, I was confronted with a caseload that was so large and staggeringly diverse that it nearly brought an immediate end to my early career. I worked across two campuses with 65 Spanish-speaking students and conducted evaluations on another five campuses. About a third of my students were in a half-day preschool program for children with disabilities. Many of my students had multiple disabilities.

I wasn't alone. The teachers I worked with had equally diverse classrooms and needed a better way to work with diverse students. The challenges of serving students from diverse backgrounds pose some of the greatest benefits and greatest difficulties of teaching. On one hand we are exposed to extremely unique and interesting cultures and the amount of impact you can make with each child is huge. On the other hand, we are never sure if a child is behind because he has not had exposure to a certain topic, is having difficulty working in a second language, or truly has a communication impairment.

I worked nights and weekends to keep up with paperwork and plan therapy and was rewarded that spring with an additional campus to cover a maternity leave. As bleak as this situation felt at the time, I now know that this a typical experience for educational professionals across the nation. These situations are challenging but they also provide us with a certain resolve and the perfect laboratory to create a solution. Speech-language pathologists and classroom teachers are able to work together to address academic goals and speech goals at the same time. The materials that lie ahead solve many of these issues by combining language enrichment strategies and academic concepts to effectively address communication disorders.

We can create materials that simultaneously enrich language skills and teach academic concepts. This way:

1) **We make no assumptions about a student's prior knowledge.**
2) **We give students multiple opportunities to practice their concepts in school and at home.**
3) **We don't waste precious time re-creating lesson plans and materials year after year.**

To solve the issue, I formed a working group with several speech pathologists to create language-rich materials and enlisted teachers from campuses across several districts to let us teach portions of the class and incorporate these language-rich materials into their classroom.

It is my hope that you find as much success with these materials as we have in supporting your teachers and moving your students through their goals.

Enjoy!

Scott Prath and the Team at Bilinguistics

HOW DO WE ENRICH LANGUAGE SKILLS THROUGHOUT THE DAY?

In order for this solution to be a success, we knew that it had to be something that could be synthesized into the current schedule of the day. That is why these language-rich lesson plans have

Attendance / Greeting	Calendar	Song
Surprise Bag	Literacy	Articulation
Phonology	Mini Books	Table Activity
Crafts	Recipe	Game

been designed around 12 common academic activities.

WHY LANGUAGE ENRICHMENT IS IMPORTANT TO TEACHERS.

Children use their language to convey what they know. Teachers are responsible for presenting a topic and then measuring whether a child has learned it or not. However, if a child does not respond or is incorrect, how do we know if:

- the topic is unfamiliar to the student
- the student knows but cannot communicate his response effectively
- the student does not know

It all looks the same right? In each instance the student has either not answered or answered incorrectly. Language-rich activities provide support so students readily share what they know.

WHY ARE CURRICULUM-BASED THEMES IMPORTANT TO SPEECH PATHOLOGISTS?

The majority of students who receive speech therapy spend thirty minutes or one hour per week with their speech therapist. This equates to three percent of a child's academic day. That means that the majority of a child's time is spent with her parents and her teacher. We also know that the more ways (multi-modal) and times (opportunities) a child practices a skill, the more she will be successful.

By using classroom themes we not only access vocabulary topics, but we also provide a way for each student to practice newly acquired communication skills on a topic that she is familiar with. Plus, the homework provides greater communication opportunities through interactions with the parent.

INTERVENTION WITH YOUNG STUDENTS IS SUCCESSFUL WHEN IT:

- Aligns to the school curriculum
- Is multi-modal
    - Hands-on, table-time, floor time
- Has buy-in from all educational professionals

- Increases parent involvement
- Can be used in a variety of settings
    - Full-day, half-day, classroom inclusion, group therapy, individual therapy
- Takes into consideration second-language influence and low socio-economic status

TEACHER INVOLVEMENT IS CRITICAL.

- Children spend the majority of their time with teachers and parents and only a small fraction of their time with speech-language pathologists.
- The value that your student places on what you are teaching dramatically increases when the same words are used by their primary communicative partners.
- Frequency and consistency are two important principles that are achieved when parents, teachers, and SLPs focus on the same topic.
- Teacher buy-in and opportunities for them to work on your student's goals are greatly enhanced when you align therapy to the school curriculum.

PARENT INVOLVEMENT IS CRITICAL.

- Parents are the most consistent language models in their children's lives.
- Parents' use of language-based strategies leads to greater receptive vocabulary at 12 years of age (Beckwith & Cohen, 1989).
- Mothers' use of labeling and increased periods of interaction leads to increases in receptive vocabulary and greater expansion of expression in older children (Tomasello & Farrar, 1986).
- Participation by fathers in early childhood programs is beneficial to the child, father and other family members (Frey, Fewell, & Vadasy, 1989; Krauss, 1993).
- Empowerment leads to self-efficacy, or the belief that parents can make a difference in their child's development (Dempsey & Dunst, 2004).
- When families are involved in the intervention process, language enrichment is ongoing rather than during "therapy" only (Rosetti, 2006).

IMPROVE ACADEMIC SUCCESS AND REDUCE SERVICE TIME.

These lesson plans were developed by a group of bilingual speech-language pathologists who provide therapy services to young children and their families through home- and school-based programs. The goal of many young classrooms is to provide early intervention in order to reduce the need for future services and improve academic outcomes later on. In this model, it is not uncommon for the speech-language pathologist to see a student in individual or group settings using therapy materials chosen solely with the child's goals in mind. While this paradigm works well for a handful of students, we found that greater gains can be made when therapy aligns to the curriculum and when parents can interact with a child based on what they bring home from school.

WHAT'S INSIDE!

HOW TO BE SUCCESSFUL.

This is not just another book of lesson plans and speech therapy ideas. We know that our success was related to *what* we used in intervention but equally important was *how* we did it. We will share with you ways to be highly successful working with young children. We begin the book with the following sections:

- Getting Started
- Preparing for each lesson plan
- Pre-session setup—Getting Ready
- Session Overview— 30 minutes at a glance
- Visual Schedule Pictures
- Explanation of visuals/schedule and how to target goals for each
- Creating a schedule and choosing your targets
- Lesson Plan Templates

ACCOUNTING FOR DIFFERENT LEARNING STYLES.

We know that different students have different learning styles and when we teach across different modalities our students have greater success. We designed each unit to address a wide range of speech and language deficits, while incorporating songs, books, and floor– and table-activities.

The content of these units was driven by theory and research in the fields of child development, communication development, and early intervention. The lessons and activities in this book are based on Vygotsky's (1967) social learning theories. Social learning theories view social interaction as critical to development. Therefore, the entire professional team is seen as the child's guides, and the child is the apprentice who learns from the adult models (Rogoff, 1990). Strategies and activities in this book are based on Kindergarten curriculum, family involvement, and group interaction (peers) so that a child's primary social interactionists are key contributors to communicative behaviors.

GETTING STARTED

The visual schedule on the following page can be reproduced to schedule your day. Print and laminate the lesson plan components. Choose the activities for the day and use them to visually show progress and completion. Each theme includes a variety of activities to provide flexibility in intervention and all components can be completed in a single day.

LESSON PLAN COMPONENTS

The first two activities, attendance/greeting and calendar, are the same for every lesson. The other activities vary according to the theme. Activities may be chosen according to the needs of the students and desired length of the lesson. The first four activities are suggested to be done with all of the students in the class. For the following activities, it is optional to split the class into groups of three or four students to rotate through the other activities. This is ideal when the teacher and/or aide is able to participate in running the activities.

It takes one or several days to complete all of the activities in each section. This works great for the classroom setting. During small group instruction or during speech therapy, open each session with the calendar and/or greetings. Then choose one to three activities and close with a review. This way, fresh activities can be completed each session while remaining on the same topic to ensure repetition of vocabulary and concepts.

Do you have children with behavioral difficulties?

Professionals who work with children who have behavior difficulties know that poor behavior can be rapidly reduced if the child is "given" control of the situation. This visual schedule allows the child to choose his preferred activity *and* the order while working on activities the professional chooses. The child's choice is still on topic but he has a sense of control in making the decision.

Components

These activities can be completed in individual sessions or in small groups.

1. Attendance/Greeting
2. Calendar
3. Song
4. Surprise Bag
5. Literacy Center
6. Articulation Station
7. Phonology Practice
8. Mini Books
9. Table Activities
10. Craft
11. Recipe
12. Game
13. Homework Sheet

www.bilinguistics.com

VISUAL SCHEDULE PICTURES

Cut out, laminate and put on a vertical Velcro strip.

Attendance/Greeting (10-20 min)

The greeting activity is completed in the same way for every lesson. Select the activities and/or prompts based on your students' goals. This can be done with all students in the circle time area. Visuals for this activity are included on the following page. Show the name of each student to the group of students and have them identify the name. The chart below shows examples of how you can target goals during this activity.

Materials: pictures and/or written names of each student, attendance board

Adult	Student	Targeted Goal
Whose name is this?	David!	*Who* questions, literacy
Where is David?	Next to Anna.	*Where* questions
What sound does "David" start with?	/d/	Phonological awareness
Let's clap out the syllables.	Da—vid	Phonological awareness
Hi David, how are you?	Fine, thanks (shakes hand)	Greetings
Are you a girl or a boy?	Boy (sticks name under boy in attendance board)	Personal information
Put your name next to/under/over the boy.	(puts name on attendance board)	Following directions, spatial concepts
What would you like me to draw for your face? (draw face by name on attendance board).	I want eyes, nose...	Requesting, sentence expansion, labeling body parts, plurals

Calendar (5-10 minutes)

The calendar activity can be completed with all students at the start of every lesson. You can review the day, month, year, and current weather.

Materials: classroom calendar, weather visual

www.bilinguistics.com

I am a boy.

I am a girl.

Soy niño.

Soy niña.

CALENDAR

Cut out, laminate and use dry erase markers to mark the dates and month.

A weather visual is included on the right page. Cut out the weather square and arrow. Poke out the two holes and use a brad to fix the arrow to the center of the weather wheel.

Curriculum-Based Speech Therapy Activities

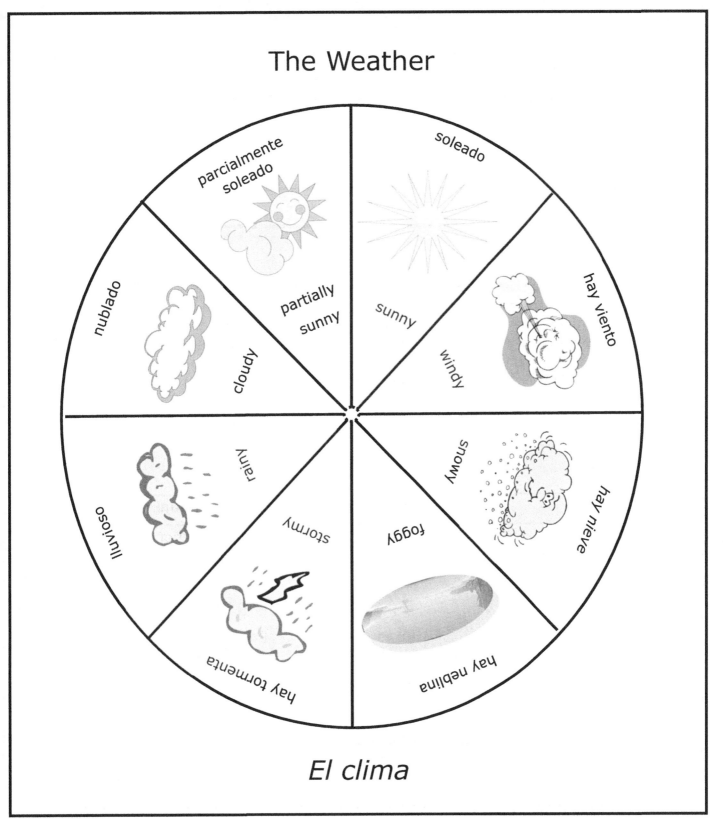

Song *(5 minutes)*

The song activity can be performed with one consistent song or songs that vary across the theme. If your group of students requires more repetition, sing the same song for every lesson. Songs about greetings, days of the week, or songs that have gestures are great choices. This activity is also a great break between seated activities. You can encourage participation by using hand signs and visual choices. If a student chooses more than one song, place the pictures on a board that says, "*first, then*."

Examples of songs are found on the first page of each unit. To find more songs and visuals that go with the songs, visit http://bilinguistics.com/music-for-speech-therapy/.

Surprise Bag *(10-15 minutes)*

The purpose of the surprise bag is to introduce the theme and any relevant vocabulary. Allow the students to sit on the floor and take turns pulling a surprise out of the surprise bag. Surprise items vary according to theme. Each chapter includes picture cards (section A of each chapter) that can be printed and cut apart for quick lesson preparation. There are also suggestions for real objects to be used with each theme.

The following is a sample script with suggested goals:

SLP	Students	Targeted Goal
Close your eyes, put your hand in, and pull out a surprise.	(pulls out a surprise)	3-step directions
Whose turn is it?	*My turn*	Requesting, turn taking, *who* questions
What would you like?	*I want to get a surprise*	Requesting, sentence expansion
What do you have?	*A fish*	Labeling
What can a fish do?	*swim*	Object function
Please put the fish on the board.	(puts the fish on the board)	1-step directions

Literacy Center *(10-15 minutes)*

This activity can be done with all students or during small group rotation. The sample chapter includes book suggestions in English and Spanish that go along with the theme, as well as the Dewey Decimal System range for a quick library stop. Read the book to the students using scaffolding techniques. If applicable, increase interactions by using surprise bag items while reading.

Optional activity:

Gather both fiction and non-fiction books to provide a variety of pictures, references, and situations. Place a number of books related to the topic on the table. Encourage students to freely pick any book, look through it, comment, trade, and show friends what they see. Tell them they have two minutes. At the end, let the group choose one book that you look through (non-fiction) or read (fiction).

Articulation Station *(5-10 minutes)*

Review and practice targets from thematic articulation words in each chapter. You may prerecord the words so your students can listen to correct models and create an auditory station to use during small group rotation. Students may color the mini book or complete other table activity worksheets while listening. You can also listen to a recorded repetitions of the target word or allow students who have mastered the sound to demonstrate.

Phonology Station *(5-10 minutes)*

Have children identify the number of syllables in each word, and practice segmenting syllables by clapping or pointing to the circles under each word. Students may also work on identifying initial sounds. This can be done with the whole class or in small groups.

Mini Books (10 min)

While sitting at a table in a small group, students can make their own mini book about the theme. Students can work on sequencing the story, following directions to put the book together, and labeling pictures in the book. There are two examples of mini books included in each section.

Table Activities (10 min)

While sitting at a table in a small group, students can complete worksheets related to the theme. Teachers might also have worksheets that relate to the theme. Collaborate with the teacher to find out what kind of materials he/she has, and work with the students in small groups to complete the worksheets. Use language scaffolding as appropriate. Hone in on specific communication goals by working together and then target individual students' goals while the others are finishing minor tasks. Allow students who have mastered a task to demonstrate to friends how to follow instructions or complete a task. There are two examples of table activities included in each section.

Crafts (15 min)

Crafts are great for students who benefit from hands-on activities. Gather the materials listed at the beginning of each session and make the minimal preparations. Empower and challenge students by having them set up for the activity. Explain what they will be doing, show an example, and them ask for helpers to gather crayons, paper, glue, etc. Increase the level of difficulty by including numbers, an order, or descriptions of the materials. This activity is great for requesting materials, following directions, sequencing, and discussing what they did using past tense verbs.

Ask the initial helpers to gather and return the materials. Have each student stand, present his work, say something about it, and carry it to their backpack, folder, or cubbie.

Recipe *(20 min)*

This is another great idea for more active students who benefit from hands-on activities. Use sequence cards and visuals to help students request materials and describe what they are doing. Finally, have them tell how they created the end product.

Game *(5-10 min)*

Games are a great way for students to be exposed to theme-based vocabulary. A file folder game is included in each section. Another great game is to go 'fishing' by tying a magnet to a piece of string tied to a stick, and using it to pick up vocabulary cards that have a paperclip on them. You can also make multiple copies of vocabulary words and play a matching game.

Parent Note

Communication growth is stimulated by carryover into the classroom, vocabulary reviews, and shared participation by a student's teacher and parents. Write a note on a theme-based coloring sheet about what you are discussing in class, and what the parents can do to work on their child's communication goals at home. Reward a student for returning a signed parent letter to encourage communication and interaction with the family.

Note: To condense your lesson plan, you may choose either a mini book, table activity, craft, recipe or game to use for the lesson plan that day. You can then use the same lesson plan several times (or have the teacher implement it) using a different activity for each day.

PREPARATION FOR EACH LESSON PLAN

PRE-SESSION SETUP

Find out what topic of the week is.

Aligning intervention themes with classroom topics increases exposure and use of vocabulary. It also provides a framework in which students can practice their new language skills. Identify what is the current academic topic for the week (E.g., oceans).

2 minutes

Go to the library and check out books on the topic.

Using books to highlight a topic can empower students by giving them experience with the topic prior to practicing the skills that you are hoping for them to gain. Gather both fiction and non-fiction books to provide vast numbers of pictures, references, and situations.

10 minutes

Copy the activity pages for each student.

Communication growth is stimulated by carryover into the classroom, vocabulary reviews, and shared participation by a student's teacher and parents. Use these friendly activities and parent letters as your communication to strengthen your team approach.

8 minutes

Cut/color/copy materials needed for each session.

These sessions were designed for fast assembly and distribution. Gather the materials listed at the beginning of each session plan and make the minimal preparations. Better yet, have your students gather and prepare their own materials and bolster their receptive communication!

10 minutes

or

no time

PREPARATION FOR EACH LESSON PLAN

SESSION OVERVIEW - 30 MINUTES AT A GLANCE

EXPRESSIVE

Book Discovery (circle time activities)

Place a number of books on the topic around the table. Encourage students to freely pick any book, look through it, comment, trade, and show friends what they see. Tell them they have two minutes. At the end, let the students choose one book that you look through (non-fiction) or read (fiction).

7 minutes

RECEPTIVE

Pre-Activity Setup

Empower and challenge students by having them set up for the activity. Explain what they will be doing, show an example, and then ask for helpers to gather crayons, paper, glue, etc. Increase the level of difficulty by including numbers, an order, or descriptions of the materials.

8 minutes

EXPRESSIVE

Activity

Hone in on specific communication goals by working together and then targeting individual student's goals while the others are finishing minor tasks. Allow successful students to demonstrate to friends how to say a sound, follow instructions, or complete a task.

18-20 minutes

RECEPTIVE

Post-Activity Review (clean up, homework)

Ask the initial helpers to gather and return the materials they brought. Have each student stand, present his work and say something about it. They can then carry it to their backpack, folder, or cubbie. Reward a student for returning a signed parent letter to encourage communication and interaction with the family.

8 minutes

Lesson Plan Template (pg. 1 of 2)

Theme: _____ Date: _____

Below is an example of a lesson plan for a 2-hour class. Modify this lesson plan as needed to fit your individual needs, including time in the classroom and student goals.

Time	Schedule	Activity	Goals
20 min. 8:30-8:50	Circle Time Greeting/ Attendance	Name recognition: Clinician holds up name card and kids find the student. Clap syllables of each name and focus on initial sounds. Clinician: **Whose name is on the card?** Students: **Jacob!** Clinician: **Where is Jacob?** Students: **Over there.** Clinician: **That's right. He is next to Keith.** **Okay, Jacob, where do I put your name? Under the boy or under the girl?** Clinician: **Okay, Jacob, what face parts do you want me to draw?** Jacob: **I want two eyes. I want a nose.**	Phoneme identification Syllables Who question Where questions Joint attention Spatial concepts Final /s/ Body parts SVO sentences
10 min. 8:50-9:00	Calendar	Go over months in a year and then dance the Macarena while singing the months. Review days of the weeks, snap the days of the week song. Review the date. **Today is X. Yesterday was X. Tomorrow will be X.**	Sequences Numbers Categories Verb tense
5 min. 9:00-9:05	Language goal	**Today, we are going to learn about _____.**	1. Label: _____ 2. Verb: _____ 3. Target questions: _____
5 min. 9:05-9:10	Music	Have the students choose between the following songs: Have the students dance the song, pairing gestures with key concepts.	Expanding utterances: "I want + to sing + ____"
15 min. 9:10-9:25	Surprise bag	Place _____ in a bag. Have the students guess what kind of animals are in the bag. **Today we are talking about _____. What do you think is in the bag?** Pass the bag around and use the same sequence instruction for each student. **Close your eyes. Put your hand in the bag. Take out your surprise.**	Naming/labeling _____ Following directions

Lesson Plan Template (pg. 2 of 2)

Theme: _____   Date:_____

Time	Activity	Description	Targets
10 min. 9:25-9:35	Phonology	**Clinician: We are also going to learn about saying sounds _____.** Review picture cards with vocabulary from book that include phonology target _____.	1. Producing words that contain the sounds:_____ _____ 2. Clapping syllables of vocabulary words
15 min. 9:35-9:50	Literacy Center	Read the book _____ Expand on what a student is saying by adding words to what he says, offering him a good example and asking him to repeat, and asking him to complete your sentence: "Clifford is a *big* _____."	Label _____ Answer WH questions SVO sentence structures
30 min. 9:50-10:20	Centers: Each group spends 15 minutes at each station (Have teacher manage one station)	**Station 1: Articulation & Listening** Review articulation cards and discuss correct articulatory placement for bilabial sounds. (10 min). Target sounds in phrases to describe the vocabulary. Children will then listen to correct models of _____ while coloring _____.	1. Sounds: _____
		Station 2: Language Activity (Choose a mini book, table activity, craft, recipe or game. You may follow the same lesson plan but vary this activity each day).	1. Labeling 2. Requesting 2. Utterance expansion 3. Following directions
10 min. 10:20-10:30	Wrap it up and clean up	Review the language target and phonological target. Have students put the parent note in their backpacks. **Today we learned about_____.** **We also talked about sounds we make _____.**	

Growing things/*Cosas que crecen*

SONGS

English	Spanish
The Garden Song	Hoy es tiempo sembrar un árbol
The Planting Song	Una semillita soy
Vegetable Song	Las verduras
Fruits Song	Las frutas
The Needs of a Plant	¿Sabes tú sembrar la col?

Songs can be found at http://bilinguistics.com/music-for-speech-therapy/.

Book and Song Resources

BOOK LOCATOR

NON-FICTION

---

580 Botanical Sciences

Title	Author
The Carrot Seed *La semilla de zanahoria*	R. Krauss
Growing Vegetable Soup *A sembrar sopa de verduras*	L. Ehlert
The Gigantic Turnip *El nabo gigante*	A. Tolstoy, N. Sharkey
Jack and the Beanstalk *Juan y los frijoles mágicos*	F. Bofill
I'm a Seed	J. Marzollo

Growing Things Unit Content

Section	Schedule	Activity	Goals
A	Surprise Bag	Cut out Growing Things cards Other options: • Plastic fruits/vegetables • Magnetic fruit/vegetables • Fruits/vegetables puzzle	• Following directions • Utterance expansion • Answering questions • Turn taking
B	Articulation Station	Garden— and growing things-related words organized by sound for articulation targets Record sounds for examples of correct productions	• Production of correct sounds in words and phrases
C	Phonology Syllable Strips	Fruit/vegetable cards in English and Spanish for 1– to 5-syllable words	• Syllable segmentation
D	Mini Book #1	What do plants need to grow? ¿Qué necesitan las plantas para crecer?	• Answering questions • Following directions • Sequencing • Utterance expansion
E	Mini Book #2	Plant a seed! ¡A sembrar una semilla!	• Following directions • Sequencing • Utterance expansion • Part-whole relationships
F	Table Activity #1	Gardening: Tools of the Trade: Matching puzzle	• Part-whole relationships • Labeling gardening tools and parts • Utterance expansion

www.bilinguistics.com

Growing Things Unit Content

Section	Schedule	Activity	Goals
G	Table Activity #2	Which is the Biggest One of All?	• Size concepts • Describing • Labeling
H	Craft #1	What's in your garden?	• Following directions • Labeling vegetables • Requesting materials
I	Craft #2	Decorate a planting pot	• Following directions • Basic concepts: part-whole, colors, number, shapes
J	Recipe	Plant a seed	• Following directions • Requesting • Sequencing • Utterance expansion
K	Game	File Folder Game: Shopping for fruits and vegetables	• Answering questions • Categorizing • Labeling • Utterance expansion
L	Parent Note	Garden coloring page	• Demonstrate learning • Give parents visual cues to understand and converse with their child

Surprise Bag:
Growing Things Picture Cards

GROWING THINGS

apple	cactus	banana	flowers
manzana	*cactus*	*plátano*	*flores*
garden	carrot	broccoli	potato
jardín	*zanahoria*	*brócoli*	*papa*
tree	tomato	leaf	lettuce
árbol	*tomate*	*hoja*	*lechuga*
corn	pineapple	beans	grass
elote	*piña*	*frijoles*	*pasto*

Articulation Station

Use these words during any of the structured activities or in homework assignments to target a child's goals.

B

GROWING THINGS

English

M   **m**ushroom, plu**m**, pu**m**pkin

P   **p**lum, **p**lant, **p**otato, **p**umpkin, **p**eas, **p**ear, **p**each, **p**ot, **p**ark

B   **b**anana, **b**roccoli, **b**lackberry, **b**ud, **b**ouquet, ca**bb**age, **b**eans

K   **c**actus, **c**arrot, **c**ucumber, **c**auliflower, **c**abbage, **k**iwi, a**c**orn

G   **g**rass, **g**row, **g**reenhouse, **g**rapes, **g**rapefruit, **g**arden, **g**round

T   **t**omato, **t**ulip, **t**ree, wa**t**er, dir**t**

D   **d**irt, **d**ig, han**d**s

F   **f**ruits, **f**lower, lea**f**

S   **s**eed**s**, **s**oil, **s**un, **s**oup, **s**prout

L   **l**ettuce, **l**eaf, **l**emon, daffodi**l**

R   **r**ain, **r**oots, **r**adish

28   Curriculum-Based Speech Therapy Activities

Articulation Station

Use these words during any of the structured activities or in homework assignments to target a child's goals.

B

GROWING THINGS

Spanish

M	**m**aíz, **m**anzana, se**m**brar, se**m**illa, **m**anos, **m**aceta
P	**p**apa, **p**epino, **p**lantar, **p**era, **p**ala, **p**asto, **p**arque
B	**b**anana, **b**rócoli, na**b**o
K	**c**omida, **k**iwi, bró**c**oli, **c**recer, **c**osechar, **c**oliflor
G	**g**uantes, gi**g**ante, a**g**ua
T	**t**omate, elo**t**e, **t**ierra
D	**d**ar, jar**d**ín, **d**urazno, ver**d**uras
F	**f**rijoles, **f**lor, a**f**uera, **f**resa, **f**rutas
S	**s**ol, **c**ebolla, **z**anahoria, **s**uelo, e**s**cavar, cre**c**er, **z**acate
L	**l**echuga, e**l**ote, árbo**l**, so**l**
R	**r**egar, na**r**anja, á**r**bol, a**r**busto, **r**aíces

www.bilinguistics.com

Phonology:
Syllable Strips in English

GROWING THINGS

corn
○

leaf
○

tree
○

apple
○ ○

flowers
○ ○

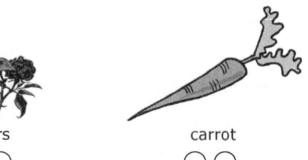
carrot
○ ○

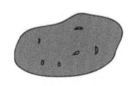
potato
○ ○ ○

banana
○ ○ ○

broccoli
○ ○ ○

tomato
○ ○ ○

pineapple
○ ○ ○

cucumber
○ ○ ○

Curriculum-Based Speech Therapy Activities

Phonology:
Syllable Strips in Spanish

GROWING THINGS

flor
○

hoja
○○

papa
○○

árbol
○○

jardín
○○

elote
○○○

tomate
○○○

brócoli
○○○

manzana
○○○

plátano
○○○

frijoles
○○○

zanahoria
○○○○

www.bilinguistics.com

Mini Book:

Cut and create a book about what plants need to grow!

D

GROWING THINGS

Plants need three things to grow.

Las plantas necesitan tres cosas para crecer.

Soil/Dirt

Tierra

Water

Agua

Sun

Sol

Mini Book:

Cut and create a book about planting a seed.

E

GROWING THINGS

Dig a hole.

Escarbe un hoyo.

Plant a seed.

Siembre una semilla.

Water the seed.

Eche agua en la semilla.

Pick the plants.

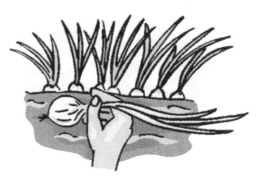

Coseche la comida.

Table Activity:

Gardening: Tools of the trade

Match the puzzle pieces to uncover gardening tools.

F

GROWING THINGS

Table Activity:

Which is the biggest one of all?

Circle the biggest vegetable in each line.

GROWING THINGS

 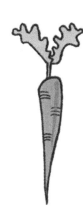 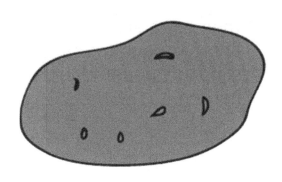

www.bilinguistics.com

Craft:
Gardening/Jardinería

H

GROWING THINGS

What's in your garden?

In this activity you will cut out food that grows in a garden. You will then cut a slit in the center of the following page and staple it to another page to make an envelope. The vegetables can then be slipped through the envelope and appear to be 'growing' in the garden.

Craft:
Gardening/Jardinería

GROWING THINGS

What's in your garden?

Craft:
Decorating a Planting Pot

Cut out the following four cards and use them as a sequencing for decorating a pot. This activity can easily be scheduled across several sessions.

I

GROWING THINGS

Gather your materials.

Junta tus materiales.

Choose your colors and paint!

¡Escoge tus colores y pinta!

Let the paint dry on your pot.

Deja que se seque la pintura.

Give it to someone you love!

¡Dásela a alguien que tú amas!

Recipe:
Plant a flower seed

GROWING THINGS

Plant a seed and watch it grow into a sunflower! You can use a cup for this activity but a good alternative is to place the soil, seeds, and water in a sandwich bag and tape it to a window. It will get a lot of sun and you can easily watch the root system develop. Remember not to seal it! Or better yet, seal one and discuss the difference in growth.

Materials: cup, soil, seeds

I want

Yo quiero

a cup

un vaso

soil

la tierra

seeds

las semillas

Recipe:
Seed Planting Sequencing

J

GROWING THINGS

Demonstrate learning or pre-teach the activity with a sequencing activity.

Put soil in the cup.

Pon tierra en el vaso.

Water the seed and put it in a sunny place.

¡Riega la semilla y ponla en un lugar soleado.

Get a cup.

Agarra un vaso.

Put the seed in the soil.

Pon la semilla en la tierra.

40   Curriculum-Based Speech Therapy Activities

Game:

File Folder Game: Shopping for fruits and vegetables

GROWING THINGS

Instructions: Enlarge pictures of shopping carts and laminate, putting five Velcro pads on each one. Cut out and laminate pictures of fruits and vegetables and attach the Velcro. Students can stick fruits in one cart and vegetables in another to practice categorizing, describing, guessing with given clues, and comparing and contrasting.

Materials: two file folders, glue, and Velcro or a sandwich bag

Game:

File Folder Game: Shopping for fruits and vegetables

GROWING THINGS

Parent Note:
Vegetable Coloring Page

GROWING THINGS

Hi Parents!

This week we are talking about growing things. Ask your child to name the vegetables and talk about where they grow.

¡Hola Padres!

Esta semana estamos hablando de cosas que crecen. Pregunten a su hijo el nombre de las verduras y dónde crecen.

www.bilinguistics.com

Food
La comida

Food/*Comida*

SONGS

English	Spanish
Apples & Bananas	*Dani—Comida*
On Top of Spaghetti	*Comida*
Do You Like Broccoli Ice Cream?	*Bombón*
Peanut Butter & Jelly	*Soy ana pizza*
Food Party	*Arroz con leche*

Songs can be found at http://bilinguistics.com/music-for-speech-therapy/.

Book and Song Resources

BOOK LOCATOR

NON-FICTION

641

Food & Drink

Title	Author
Stone Soup *Sopa de piedras*	M. Brown
The Gigantic Turnip *El nabo gigante*	A. Tolstoy & N. Sharkey
The Very Hungry Caterpillar *La oruga muy hambrienta*	E. Carle
The Gingerbread Man *El hombre de pan de jengibre*	C. McCafferty

Food Unit Content

Section	Schedule	Activity	Goals
A	Surprise Bag	Cut out food picture cards Other options: • Plastic toy foods • Real foods	• Following directions • Utterance expansion • Answering questions • Turn taking
B	Articulation Station	Food-related words organized by sound for articulation targets Record sounds for examples of correct productions	• Production of correct sounds in words and phrases
C	Phonology Syllable Strips	Food picture cards in English and Spanish for 1- to 4-syllable words	• Syllable segmentation
D	Mini Book #1	Where Food Comes From ¿De Dónde Viene La Comida?	• Answering questions • Following directions • Sequencing • Utterance expansion
E	Mini Book #2	What Do You Eat? ¿Qué Comes?	• Following directions • Sequencing • Utterance expansion • Part-whole relationships
F	Table Activity #1	Part and Whole Relationships	• Part-whole relationships • Labeling foods and parts • Utterance expansion

Food Unit Content

Section	Schedule	Activity	Goals
G	Table Activity #2	Which is the Smallest Food of All?	• Size concepts • Describing • Labeling
H	Craft #1	Super Silly Pizza	• Following directions • Labeling foods • Requesting materials
I	Craft #2	Fruit Loops Necklace	• Following directions • Basic concepts: part-whole, colors, number, shapes
J	Recipe	Making Fruit Salad	• Following directions • Requesting • Sequencing • Utterance expansion
K	Game	File Folder Game: Foods	• Answering questions • Categorizing • Labeling • Utterance expansion
L	Parent Note	Food Coloring Page	• Demonstrate learning • Give parents visual cues to understand and converse with their child

Surprise Bag: Food Picture Cards

A
FOOD

bread	watermelon	pizza	soup
pan	*sandía*	*pizza*	*sopa*
cheese	grapes	potato	cookie
queso	*uvas*	*papa*	*galleta*
apple	tomato	broccoli	taco
manzana	*tomate*	*brócoli*	*taco*
ice cream	burger	salad	strawberry
helado	*hamburguesa*	*ensalada*	*fresa*

www.bilinguistics.com

Articulation Station

Use these words during any of the structured activities or in homework assignments to target a child's goals.

B

FOOD

English

M	**m**eat, **m**ilk, **m**ango, **m**elon, **m**uffin, le**m**on, to**m**ato, ha**m**
P	**p**izza, **p**lum, **p**eas, **p**ear, **p**otato, **p**asta, ap**p**le, cantalou**p**e
B	**b**anana, **b**read, **b**eans, **b**acon, **b**urger, **b**roccoli, **b**reakfast
K	**c**ake, **c**ookie, **c**ucumber, chi**ck**en, **c**offee, **c**andy, **c**antaloupe
G	**g**rapes, ba**g**el, e**gg**, hotdo**g**, bur**g**er, **g**reen beans, spa**gh**etti
T	**t**oast, **t**omato, **t**una, **t**ortilla, **t**ater **t**o**ts**, **t**aco
D	**d**onut, **d**inner, hot**d**og, noo**d**les, can**d**y
F	**f**ish, co**ff**ee, **f**ruit, mu**ff**in, **f**ajitas, **f**rench **f**ries
S	**s**oup, **s**alad, jui**c**e, **s**trawberry, **s**au**s**age, pa**s**ta, **s**paghetti
L	**l**emon, **l**ettuce, **l**unch, me**l**on, p**l**um, app**l**e, brocco**l**i, nood**l**e
R	**r**ice, **r**aspe**rr**y, **r**adish, f**r**uit, b**r**ead, b**r**occoli, to**r**tilla, g**r**apes

50   Curriculum-Based Speech Therapy Activities

Articulation Station

FOOD

Use these words during any of the structured activities or in homework assignments to target a child's goals.

Spanish

M	**m**iel, **m**elón, **m**ango, **m**anzana, ja**m**ón, co**m**ida, li**m**ón
P	**p**an, **p**apas, **p**era, **p**epino, **p**iña, **p**ollo, so**p**a, **p**izza, **p**escado
B	**b**istec, **b**ocadillo, rá**b**ano, **b**rócoli, al**b**óndigas
K	**c**arne, azú**c**ar, ta**c**o, **c**afé, **c**oca, **q**ueso, **c**aramelo, **q**uesadilla
G	**g**alleta, ju**g**o, **g**arbanzos, **g**uisantes, espárra**g**os, lechu**g**a
T	**t**aco, **t**omate, a**t**ún, **t**ortilla, **t**ostado, acei**t**e, melocó**t**ón
D	**d**ona, **d**ulce, **d**esayuno, comi**d**a, cal**d**o, pesca**d**o, ensala**d**a
F	**f**resa, **f**lan, **f**ruta, **f**rijoles, ca**f**é, **f**rambuesa
S	**s**andía, **s**opa, **s**al**s**a, que**s**o, **s**alchicha, pe**s**cado, man**z**ana
L	**l**eche, **l**imón, **l**echuga, sa**l**, **l**entejas, me**l**ón, carame**l**o, ensa**l**ada
R	**r**ico, **r**ábano, pe**r**a, ca**r**amelo, f**r**uta, b**r**ócoli, ca**r**ne, ci**r**uela

Phonology:
Syllable Strips in English

FOOD

egg
○

cake
○

bread
○

taco
○○

pizza
○○

cookie
○○

tomato
○○○

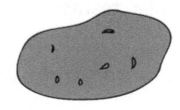

potato
○○○

banana
○○○

spaghetti
○○○

strawberry
○○○

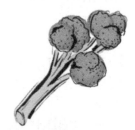

broccoli
○○○

Phonology:
Syllable Strips in Spanish

FOOD

pan
○

pastel
○ ○

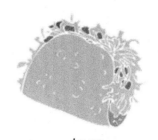

taco
○ ○

pizza
○ ○

tomate
○ ○ ○

galleta
○ ○ ○

sandía
○ ○ ○

brócoli
○ ○ ○

helado
○ ○ ○

hamburgesa
○ ○ ○ ○

ensalada
○ ○ ○ ○

zanahoria
○ ○ ○ ○

www.bilinguistics.com

Mini Book:

Cut, color, and create a *WHERE* book about food.

D

FOOD

Where does food come from?

¿De dónde viene la comida?

Milk comes from cows.

La leche viene de las vacas.

Vegetables come from the ground.

Los vegetales vienen de la tierra.

Meat comes from animals.

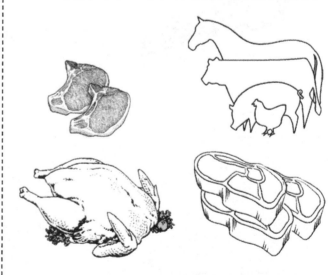

La carne viene de los animales.

Mini Book:

Cut, color, and create a book about food.

FOOD

Which foods do you eat?

¿Cuáles comidas comes?

Which fruits do you eat?

¿Cuáles frutas comes?

Which meats do you eat?

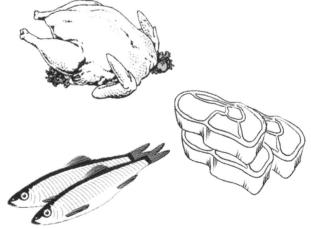

¿Cuáles carnes comes?

Which vegetables do you eat?

¿Cuáles vegetales comes?

www.bilinguistics.com

Table Activity:
Part-Whole Relationships

Match the food to the part and color if time permits.

FOOD

Table Activity:

Which is the smallest in each row?

Circle the smallest food in each line.

FOOD

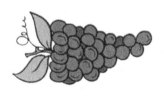

www.bilinguistics.com

Craft:
Super Silly Pizza

Cut, color, and glue funny foods onto the pizza.

Materials: scissors, tape, crayons

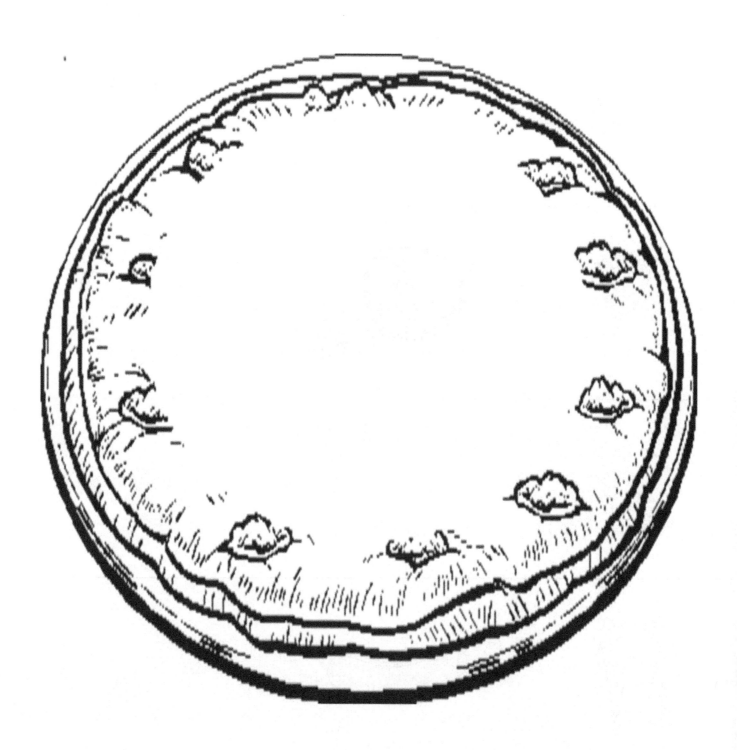

 # Craft:
Super Silly Pizza

FOOD

Craft:
Fruit Loop Necklace

FOOD

Use Fruit Loops in a jar as a token-reinforcer. When the jar is full (or when you decide they are ready), student can request pieces to string onto their necklaces.

Materials: Fruit Loops (or another thread-able snack), string

Recipe:
Making Fruit Salad

FOOD

Cut up common fruits and use the activity as an opportunity to have students choose the fruits that they like best, mix flavors, and request more.

Materials: bowl, knife, spoon, bananas, oranges, strawberries, or fruits of your choice

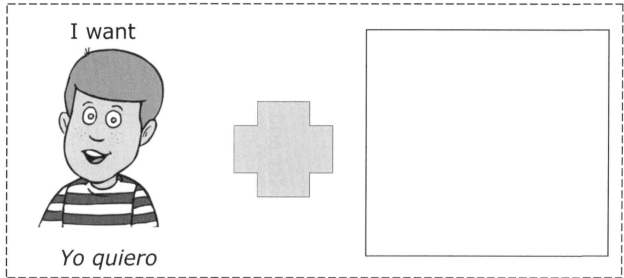

www.bilinguistics.com

Recipe:
Making Fruit Salad

J — FOOD

Get a spoon.

Agarra una cuchara.

Mix and eat the fruit.

¡Mezcla y come la fruta!

Get a bowl.

Agarra un tazón.

Put the fruit in the bowl.

Pon la fruta en el tazón.

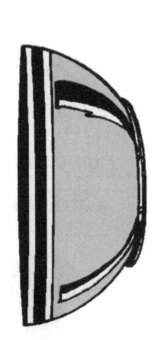

Game:

File Folder Game: Animal Foods

FOOD

Cut out and paste the page of animals on the inside of a file folder. Use Velcro, putty, or tape, to stick food pictures from a grab-bag to the animal that eats that food.

Note: Animal pictures will cover one page of the inside of the file folder. Use the other inside page to mount the foods on Velcro or tape a baggie to keep the foods inside.

Materials: one file folder, glue, and Velcro or a sandwich bag.

*Bonus—as the children match each food to the animal that eats it, ask if it is a food that people eat too. Ex: "I eat carrots, and so do rabbits!" "I don't eat flies, but frogs do!"

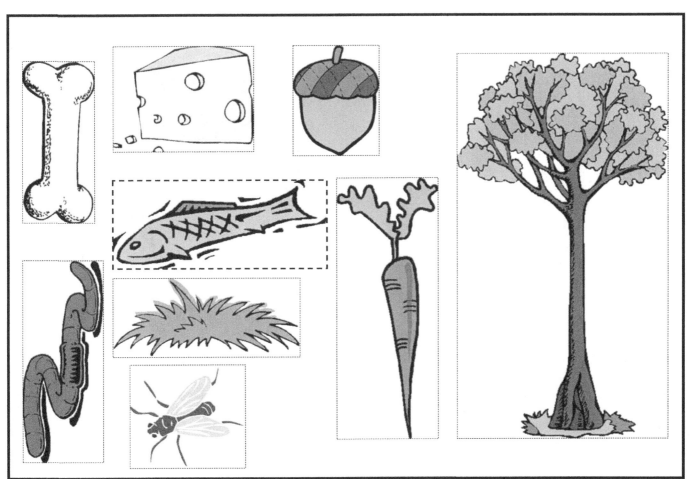

www.bilinguistics.com

Game:
File Folder Game: Animal Foods

Game:
File Folder Game: Animal Foods

Game:

File Folder Game: Animal Foods

FOOD

Parent Note:
Food Coloring Page

Hi Parents!

This week we are talking about foods. Ask your child to share what he knows about the food that you have in your house.

¡Hola Padres!

Esta semana estamos hablando de las comidas. Platiquen con su hijo sobre los alimentos que tienen en su casa.

www.bilinguistics.com

Weather
El clima

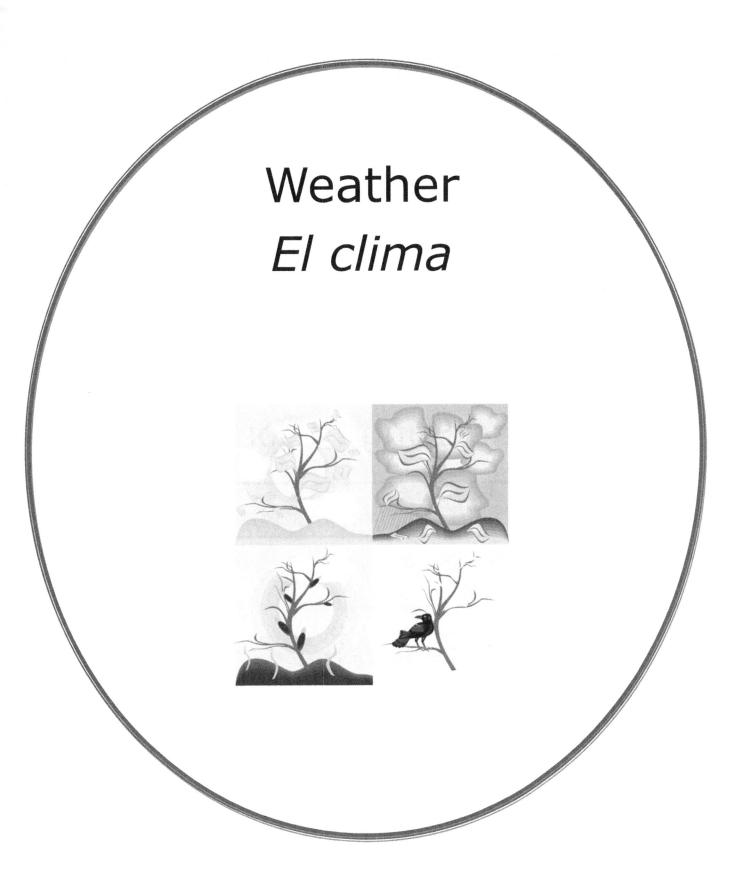

Weather / El clima

SONGS

English	Spanish
How's the Weather?	¿Cómo está el clima?
It's Rainy	Que llueva, que llueva
Weather Helper Song	Las hojitas
The Weather	Witsi witsi araña
My Raincoat	El chorrito

Songs can be found at http://bilinguistics.com/music-for-speech-therapy/.

Book and Song Resources

BOOK LOCATOR

NON-FICTION

Sciences/Weather

Title	Author
The Weather *El tiempo*	G. Rosa-Mendoza
What Should I Wear Today? *¿Qué ropa me pongo hoy?*	J. Kondrchek
Bear in Sunshine *Oso bajo sol*	S. Blackstone
Elmer's Weather *Elmer y el tiempo*	D. McKee
Iguanas in the Snow *Iguanas en la nieve*	F. Alarcon
The Lizard and the Sun *La lagartija y el sol*	A. Ada

Weather Unit Content

Section	Schedule	Activity	Goals
A	Surprise Bag	Cut out weather picture cards Other options: • Cotton balls as clouds • Ice in a baggie (as hail)	• Following directions • Utterance expansion • Answering questions • Turn taking
B	Articulation Station	Weather-related words organized by sound for articulation targets Record sounds for examples of correct productions	• Production of correct sounds in words and phrases
C	Phonology Syllable Strips	Weather picture cards in English and Spanish for 1– to 5-syllable words	• Syllable segmentation
D	Mini Book #1	Weather in Seasons *El clima de las estaciones*	• Answering questions • Following directions • Sequencing • Utterance expansion
E	Mini Book #2	Help Me Dress for the Weather *Ayúdame a vestirme para el clima*	• Following directions • Sequencing • Utterance expansion
F	Table Activity #1	Matching	• Matching • Labeling weather and clothes • Utterance expansion

Weather Unit Content

Section	Schedule	Activity	Goals
G	Table Activity #2	What clothes should I wear?	• Utterance expansion • Describing • Labeling clothes and weather
H	Craft #1	Weather Mobile	• Following directions • Labeling weather • Requesting materials
I	Craft #2	Make a Rainbow	• Following directions • Basic concepts: describing different textures, colors, shapes • Requesting
J	Recipe	Make Your Own Tornado	• Following directions • Requesting • Sequencing • Utterance expansion
K	Game	File Folder Game: Dress Me	• Answering questions • Categorizing • Labeling • Utterance expansion
L	Parent Note	Weather Coloring Page	• Demonstrate learning • Give parents visual cues to understand and converse with their child

Surprise Bag: Weather Picture Cards

WEATHER

rainy	cloudy	tornado	sunny
lluvioso	*nublado*	*tornado*	*asoleado*
rainbow	seasons	wind	storm
arco iris	*estaciones*	*viento*	*tormenta*
summer	winter	fall	spring
verano	*invierno*	*otoño*	*primavera*
hurricane	snow	lightning	thermometer
huracán	*nieve*	*relámpago*	*termómetro*

www.bilinguistics.com

# Articulation Station

Use these words during any of the structured activities or in homework assignments to target a child's goals.

WEATHER

English

M stor**m**, **m**ist, **m**uggy, war**m**, cli**m**ate, da**m**p

P dam**p**, down**p**our,

B **b**lizzard, lightning **b**olt, **b**reeze

K **c**limate, **c**loudy, **c**old, hurri**c**ane, over**c**ast, soa**k**ed

G fo**g**, **g**ust of wind, fo**g**,

T s**t**orm, fros**t**, hails**t**ones, ligh**t**ning, drough**t**, hea**t**, mis**t**, **t**ornado, forecas**t**, **t**emperature, mis**t**y, ho**t**, clima**t**e

D **d**rizzle, **d**ownpour, **d**renched, thun**d**er, clou**d**, **d**ew, col**d**, clou**d**y, torna**d**o, win**d**, **d**rought

F **f**og, **f**lurry, **f**rost, **f**orecast, **f**lood, **f**reezing

S **s**unny, ice, mi**s**ty, overca**s**t, **s**torm, **s**now, **s**lush, **s**leet, **s**oaked

L drizz**l**e, f**l**urry, s**l**eet, hai**l**, b**l**izzard, bo**l**t of **l**ightning, c**l**oud, co**l**d, f**l**ood, c**l**imate

R thunde**r**, wa**r**m, to**r**nado, weathe**r**, d**r**ought, showe**r**, d**r**izzle, **r**ain, flu**rr**y, downpou**r**, f**r**ost, sto**r**m, b**r**eeze, hu**rr**icane, tempe**r**ature, ove**r**cast, ai**r**

Articulation Station

Use these words during any of the structured activities or in homework assignments to target a child's goals.

B

WEATHER

Spanish

M	**m**ono de nieve, relá**m**pago, tor**m**enta, cli**m**a, te**m**peratura, hú**m**edo
P	relám**p**ago, em**p**a**p**ado, tem**p**eratura
B	**b**risa, nie**b**la, nu**b**e, nie**v**e, llu**v**ia, llo**v**izna, **v**iento
K	**c**alor, **c**lima, se**c**o, hura**c**án
G	**g**ranizo, relámpa**g**o, ráfa**g**a, a**g**uanieve, **g**ris
T	**t**ormenta, **t**rueno, **t**emperatura, **t**ornado, **t**iempo, **t**emplado, vien**t**o, es**t**ación, nieve derre**t**ida
D	hela**d**o, torna**d**o, templa**d**o, húme**d**o, nieve **d**erretida
F	**f**rio, rá**f**aga
S	grani**z**o, llovi**z**na, bri**s**a, inunda**c**ión, caluro**s**o, **s**eco, lluvio**s**o, nebulo**s**o, **s**ol, **s**oleado, vento**s**o
L	re**l**ámpago, nub**l**arse, nieb**l**a, he**l**ado, hie**l**o, ca**l**or, ca**l**uroso, c**l**ima, temp**l**ado, nebu**l**oso
R	**r**áfaga, llove**r**, g**r**anizo, neva**r**, to**r**menta, nieve de**rr**etida, t**r**ueno, nublar**s**e, b**r**isa, calo**r**, f**r**io, hu**r**acán, tempe**r**atura

www.bilinguistics.com

Phonology: Syllable Strips in English

C WEATHER

snow
○

rain
○

wind
○

rainbow
○ ○

lightning
○ ○

snowflake
○ ○

jacket
○ ○

seasons
○ ○

thunderstorm
○ ○ ○

tornado
○ ○ ○

hurricane
○ ○ ○

thermometer
○ ○ ○ ○

Curriculum-Based Speech Therapy Activities

Phonology:
Syllable Strips in Spanish

WEATHER

nieve
○○

nube
○○

viento
○○

lluvia
○○

verano
○○○

invierno
○○○

tornado
○○○

huracán
○○○

tormenta
○○○

relámpago
○○○○

arco iris
○○○○

temperatura
○○○○○

www.bilinguistics.com

Mini Book:

Cut, color, and create a book about weather.

WEATHER

Weather in Seasons

El clima de las estaciones

The weather is cold in the winter.

El clima es frío en el invierno.

The weather is rainy in the spring.

El clima es lluvioso en la primavera.

The weather is hot in the summer.

El clima es caliente en el verano.

Mini Book:
Cut, color, and create a book about weather.

WEATHER

Draw my umbrella!

Help Me Dress for the Weather!

¡Ayúdame a vestirme para el clima!

¡Dibuja mi paraguas!

Draw my sunglasses.

Draw my jacket. I'm cold!

Dibuja mis lentes del sol.

Dibuja mi chaqueta. ¡Tengo frío!

www.bilinguistics.com

Table Activity:

Matching

Match the season to the weather and color if time permits.

WEATHER

Table Activity:

What clothes should I wear?

Circle the clothes in each line that go best with the weather.

WEATHER

Craft:
Weather Mobile

WEATHER

Cut, color, and connect these types of weather into a weather mobile. The easiest way is to tape the string to the back of each picture.

Materials: scissors, 7 pieces of string, tape, crayons

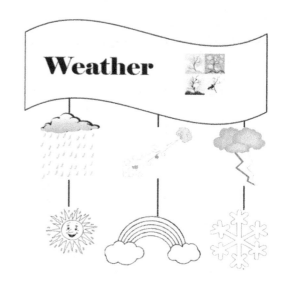

82   Curriculum-Based Speech Therapy Activities

Craft:
Weather Mobile

WEATHER

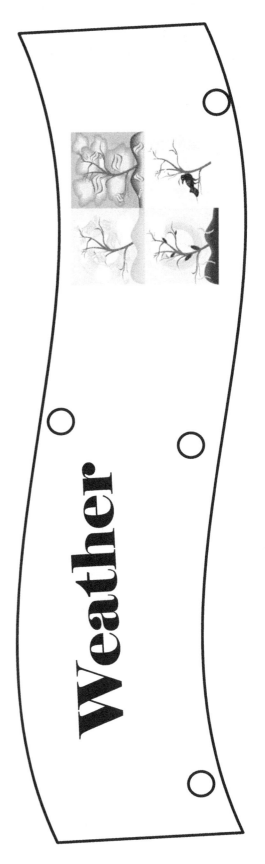

Weather

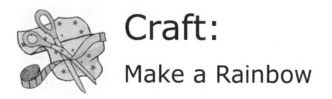

Craft:
Make a Rainbow

WEATHER

Be as creative and as colorful as you want! Use this template as a guide to make your own rainbows. Add different textures to each color and have child describe what he feels.

Materials: cotton balls, glue, construction paper, different textures (i.e. froot loops, crayon shavings, glitter, construction paper, painted macaroni, tissue paper, etc.) in red, orange, yellow, green, blue, purple

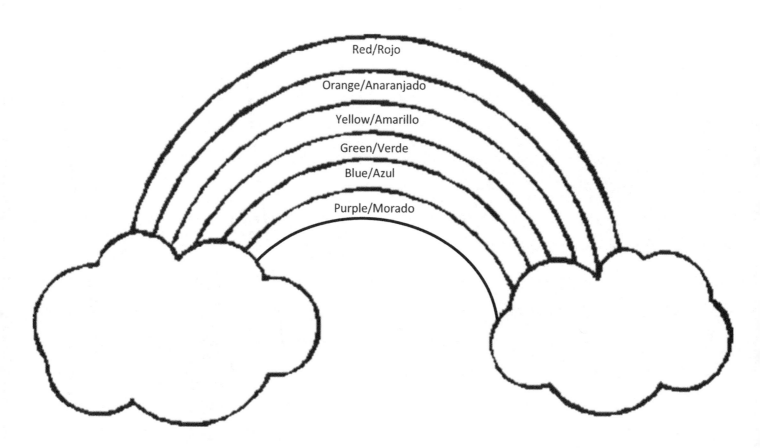

Recipe:
Make Your Own Tornado

WEATHER

Demonstrate how a tornado forms to increase your students' interest in weather patterns. Then use the activity to take turns, identify colors, follow directions, and describe outcomes.

Materials: 2 bottles, water (enough for 3/4 of the bottle), food coloring, and tape

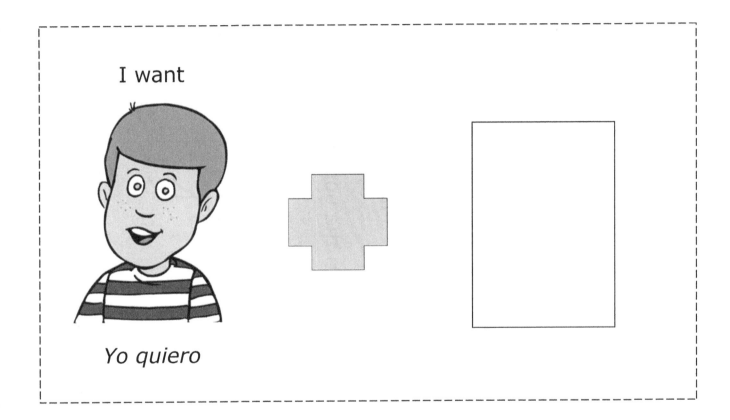

I want

Yo quiero

2 bottles

2 botellas

water

agua

food coloring

pintura de comida

tape

cinta adhesiva

www.bilinguistics.com

Recipe:
Make Your Own Tornado

WEATHER

Demonstrate learning or pre-teach the activity with a sequencing activity.

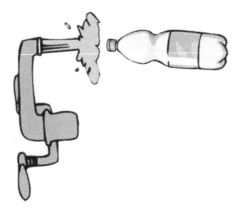

Put water and coloring in the bottle.

Pon agua y color en la botella.

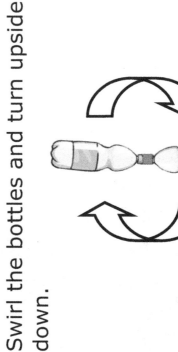

Swirl the bottles and turn upside down.

Gira el agua y voltéalas de cabeza.

Get 2 bottles.

Agarra dos botellas.

Tape second bottle to the top.

Pega la otra botella arriba con cinta.

Game:

File Folder Game: Dress Me

WEATHER

Cut out and paste pictures on the inside of a file folder. Use Velcro or putty to stick clothing pictures to the correct weather scene (cold, rainy, hot).

Materials: 2 file folders, glue Velcro or a baggie

Note: Pictures will cover one and a half pages of the inside of the file folder. Use the extra room on the half page to mount the clothes on Velcro or tape a baggie to keep the clothes inside.

Game:
File Folder Game: Dress Me

WEATHER

Game:
File Folder Game: Dress Me

WEATHER

Parent Note:
Weather Coloring Page

WEATHER

Hi Parents! This week we are talking about weather. Take turns rolling the weather die and ask your child to talk about different climates and the clothing you need when the weather changes.

¡Hola Padres! Esta semana estamos hablando del clima. Tomen turnos rodando el dado y platiquen con su hijo sobre los climas diferentes y la ropa que se usa en cada clima.

Places We Go
Lugares donde vamos

Places We Go / *Lugares donde vamos*

SONGS

English	Spanish
Wheels on the Bus	*Las ruedas del autobús*
Row Row Row Your Boat	*Vamos a remar*
'Oh The Places you'll Go' by Dr Seuss (Tim Moore)	*Me gusta viajar (Toobys)*
The Ants Go Marching	*Las hormigas marchan*
Goodbye Friends	*Adiós mis amigos*

Songs can be found at http://bilinguistics.com/music-for-speech-therapy/.

Book and Song Resources

BOOK LOCATOR

NON-FICTION

910 Geography and Travel

Title	Author
Bear About Town / *Oso en la ciudad*	S. Blackstone
I Went Walking / *Salí de paseo*	S. Williams
If You Take a Mouse to School / *Si llevas un ratón a escuela*	L. Numeroff
This Is the Way We Go to School: A Book About Children Around the World	E. Baer
Oh, the Places You'll Go! / *¡Oh, cúan lejos llegarás!*	Dr. Seuss

Places We Go Unit Content

Section	Schedule	Activity	Goals
A	Surprise Bag	Cut out picture cards of the various places Other options: • Photos of familiar places n the community • Doll house furniture	• Following directions • Utterance expansion • Answering questions • Turn taking
B	Articulation Station	'Place-related words organized by sound for articulation targets Record sounds for examples of correct productions	• Production of correct sounds in words and phrases
C	Phonology Syllable Strips	'Places' picture cards in English and Spanish for 1– to 4-syllable words	• Syllable segmentation
D	Mini Book #1	The Places I Go ¿A dónde voy?	• Answering questions • Following directions • Sequencing • Utterance expansion
E	Mini Book #2	I'm Going Shopping! ¡Voy de compras!	• Following directions • Sequencing • Utterance expansion
F	Table Activity #1	Where Does It Belong?	• Categories • Labeling foods and locations • Utterance expansion

Places We Go Unit Content

Section	Schedule	Activity	Goals
G	Table Activity #2	Which Item Does Not Belong?	• Categories • Describing • Labeling
H	Craft #1	Build a House	• Following directions • Labeling • Requesting materials
I	Craft #2	Create a City	• Following directions • Labeling places • Utterance expansion • Requesting materials
J	Recipe	Bubble Wrap Starfish	• Following directions • Requesting • Sequencing • Utterance expansion
K	Game	File Folder Game: Places We Go	• Answering questions • Categorizing • Labeling • Utterance expansion
L	Parent Note	Places We Go Coloring Page	• Demonstrate learning • Give parents visual cues to understand and converse with their child

Surprise Bag: Places Picture Cards

PLACES

library	post office	airport	hospital
biblioteca	*correo*	*aeropuerto*	*hospital*
restaurant	bakery	park	veterinarian
restaurante	*panadería*	*parque*	*veterinario*
city	country	house	school
ciudad	*campo*	*casa*	*escuela*
store	beach	mall	movie theater
tienda	*playa*	*plaza comercial*	*cine*

www.bilinguistics.com

Articulation Station

Use these words during any of the structured activities or in homework assignments to target a child's goals.

PLACES

English

M   **m**ountains, **m**all, **m**ovie theater

P   **p**ost office, **p**ool, **p**ark, **p**olice, air**p**ort, hos**p**ital

B   **b**akery, **b**each, neigh**b**orhood, li**b**rary

K   **c**ountry, ba**k**ery, par**k**

G   **g**as station

T   hospi**t**al, restauran**t**, ci**t**y, coun**t**ry, **s**tore, **s**tation, fores**t**, moun**t**ains, deser**t**, ve**t**, pos**t** office, airpor**t**, gas **s**tation

D   **d**esert

F   **f**ire station, **f**orest

S   **s**ity, **s**chool, **s**tore, **s**tation, de**s**ert, fore**st**, mountain**s**, hou**s**e, po**s**t office, ho**s**pital

L   **l**ibrary, hospita**l**, schoo**l**, po**l**ice station, hair sa**l**on

R   **r**estaurant, bake**r**y, pa**r**k, count**r**y, sto**r**e, fi**r**e station, fo**r**est, dese**r**t, neighbo**r**hood, lib**r**ary, ai**r**port, hai**r** salon

Curriculum-Based Speech Therapy Activities

# Articulation Station

Use these words during any of the structured activities or in homework assignments to target a child's goals.

PLACES

Spanish

M **m**all, ca**m**po, plaza co**m**ercial

P **p**anadero, **p**laya, **p**olicía, **p**arque, cam**p**o, aero**p**uerto, hos**p**ital

B **b**iblioteca, **b**ombero, **v**eterinario, al**b**erca

K **c**asa, **c**orreo, **c**afé, **c**ampo, biblio**c**a, par**q**ue, es**c**uela, alber**c**a

G **g**asolinera

T **t**ienda, biblio**t**eca, aeropuer**t**o, hospi**t**al, ve**t**erinario, es**t**ación

D pana**d**ero, ciu**d**ad

F ca**f**é

S **c**iudad, **c**ine, ho**s**pital, ca**s**a, e**s**cuela, e**s**tación, poli**c**ía, bombero**s**

L bib**l**ioteca, hospita**l**, escue**l**a, p**l**aya, po**l**icía, a**l**berca

R co**rr**eo, ae**r**opuerto, panade**r**o, albe**r**ca, pa**r**que, vete**r**ina**r**io, bombe**r**os

Phonology:
Syllable Strips in English

C PLACES

store
◯

park
◯

house
◯

airport
◯ ◯

mountains
◯ ◯

ocean
◯ ◯

library
◯ ◯ ◯

neighborhood
◯ ◯ ◯

bakery
◯ ◯ ◯

hospital
◯ ◯ ◯

fire station
◯ ◯ ◯

police station
◯ ◯ ◯ ◯

Phonology:
Syllable Strips in Spanish

C

PLACES

casa
○ ○

campo
○ ○

café
○ ○

playa
○ ○

parque
○ ○

tienda
○ ○

escuela
○ ○ ○

ciudad
○ ○ ○

correo
○ ○ ○

estación
○ ○ ○

panadero
○ ○ ○ ○

veterinario
○ ○ ○ ○ ○

www.bilinguistics.com

Mini Book:

Cut, color, and create a *WHERE* book about places.

PLACES

I live in a _____.

The Places I Go

¿A dónde voy?

Yo vivo en un(a) _____.

I shop in a _____.

Compro cosas en una _____.

I play at the _____.

Yo juego en el _____.

Mini Book:

Cut, color, and create a book about going to the grocery store.

PLACES

I'm Going Shopping!

¡Voy de compras!

I make a shopping list.

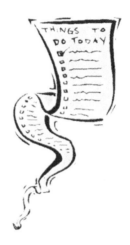

Hago una lista de compras.

I go to the store and get a cart.

Voy a la tienda y agarro un carrito.

I find the food on my list.

Encuentro la comida en mi lista.

www.bilinguistics.com

Table Activity:
Where Does It Belong?

PLACES — F

Draw a line from the item on the left to the place on the right where the item belongs.

Table Activity:
Which Item Does Not Belong?

Circle the item that does not go with the other two in the line.

PLACES

www.bilinguistics.com

Craft:
Build a House!

PLACES

Stuff a paper bag and glue it onto a green sheet of paper. Cut out the images for the roof, windows, chimney and door and glue them onto the paper bag to create a house.

Materials: scissors, paper bag, green paper, images of windows, door, roof and chimney, glue, something to stuff the paper bag

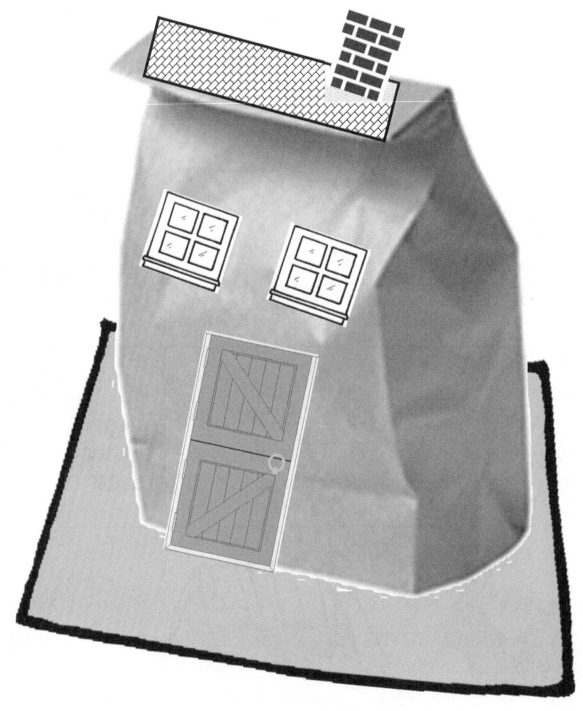

Craft:
Build a House!

PLACES

www.bilinguistics.com

Craft:
Create a City

PLACES

Draw or paint a road or multiple roads on a large piece of paper. Enlarge the pictures of places found below and glue them along the road to create a city. Students can 'drive' through the city and/or take turns telling other students where to go. For example: 'Drive to the park.' 'Go to school."

Materials: large sheet of paper, markers or paint, glue, toy car, enlarged pictures of places we can go

Craft:
Create a City

I PLACES

Recipe:
Bubble Wrap Starfish

PLACES

Make a starfish craft to expand on students' knowledge of the beach. Use the activity to take turns, make requests, identify colors, follow directions, and describe outcomes.

Materials: colored paper, bubble wrap, paint

I want

Yo quiero

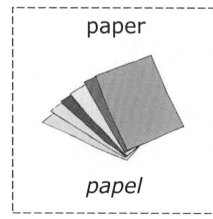

paper

papel

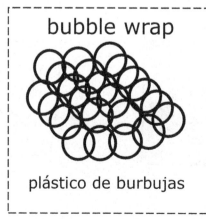

bubble wrap

plástico de burbujas

paint

pintura

Recipe:
Bubble Wrap Starfish Sequencing

J **PLACES**

Demonstrate learning or pre-teach the activity with a sequencing activity.

Select a color of paint.

Es- Select a color of paint.

Use the painted bubble wrap as a stamp on the colored paper to make a starfish.

Usa el plástico de burbujas como sello sobre papel para hacer una estrella del mar.

Select a piece of colored paper.

Agarra un papel de color.

Paint the bubble side of the bubble wrap that has been cut into the shape of a star.

Pinta el plástico de burbujas (previamente cortado en forma de una estrella) del lado de las burbujas.

www.bilinguistics.com

Game:
File Folder Game: Places We Go

PLACES

Cut out and paste pictures of places on the inside of a file folder. Use Velcro or putty to stick the various items included on the next page (ex. scissors, towel, milk) to the correct places (grocery store, pool, school).

Materials: one file folder, glue and Velcro or a baggie

Note: Pictures will cover one and a half pages of the inside of the file folder. Use the extra room on the half page to mount the items on Velcro or tape a baggie to keep the items inside the folder.

 # Game:
File Folder Game: Places We Go

PLACES

www.bilinguistics.com

Game:
File Folder Game: Places We Go

PLACES

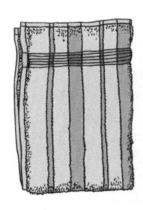   

Parent Note:
Places We Go

PLACES

Hi Parents!

This week we are talking about places we go. Ask your child to share what he knows about the places in the scene below and talk about what you do at the various places.

¡Hola Padres!

Esta semana estamos hablando de los lugares que visitamos. Platiquen con su hijo sobre lugares donde van y que hacen en estos lugares.

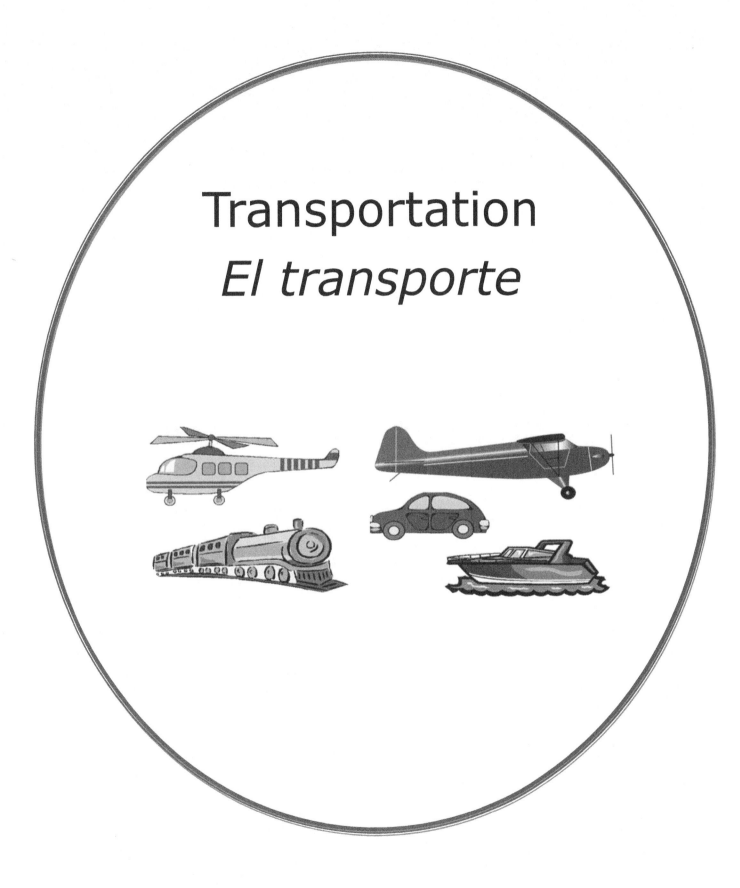

Transportation / *El transporte*

SONGS

English	Spanish
The Wheels on the Bus	*Las ruedas del autobús*
Row Row Row your Boat	*Rema tu bote*
Down by the Station	*En la estación*
I'm a Little Piece of Tin	*Saludando al tren*
Little Red Caboose	*Había una vez un avión*

Songs can be found at http://bilinguistics.com/music-for-speech-therapy/.

Book and Song Resources

BOOK LOCATOR

NON-FICTION

385-388 Transportation

Title	Author
Bear on a Bike / *Oso en bicicleta*	S. Blackstone
The Journey Home from Grandpa's	J. Lumley
We All Go Traveling By	S. Roberts
I Wish I Were a Pilot	S. Blackstone
El baul de los transportes. Un libro sobre	C. Pisos
Transportation— Medios de transporte (Bilingual Book)	S. Liebermann

Transportation Unit Content

Section	Schedule	Activity	Goals
A	Surprise Bag	Cut out transportation picture cards Other options: plastic toy airplanes, cars, etc.	• Following directions • Utterance expansion • Answering questions • Turn taking
B	Articulation Station	Transportation-related words organized by sound for articulation targets Record sounds for examples of correct productions	• Production of correct sounds in words and phrases
C	Phonology Syllable Strips	Transportation picture cards in English and Spanish for 1- to 5-syllable words	• Syllable segmentation
D	Mini Book #1	Where do we travel? ¿Dónde viajamos?	• Answering questions • Following directions • Sequencing • Utterance expansion
E	Mini Book #2	Who travels? ¿Quién viaja?	• Following directions • Sequencing • Utterance expansion • Part-whole relationships
F	Table Activity #1	"Which vehicles are biggest and smallest?" academic activity	• Size and shapes • Labeling vehicles • Utterance expansion

www.bilinguistics.com

Transportation Unit Content

Section	Schedule	Activity	Goals
G	Table Activity #2	"Which vehicle travels on land?" academic activity	• Categorizing • Describing • Labeling
H	Craft #1	Train Construction: Visuospatial shape learning activity	• Following directions • Shapes • Requesting materials
I	Craft #2	Sea and Sky: Color shapes and produce prepositional phrases	• Following directions • Basic concepts: colors, number, shapes • Requesting materials
J	Recipe	Traffic Light: Made with graham crackers, peanut butter and red, yellow, and green apples	• Following directions • Requesting • Sequencing • Utterance expansion
K	Game	File Folder Game: Where do vehicles travel?	• Answering questions • Categorizing • Labeling • Utterance expansion
L	Parent Note	Transportation coloring page	• Demonstrate learning • Give parents visual cues to understand and converse with their child

Surprise Bag:
Transportation Picture Cards

A

TRANSPORTATION

car	airplane	bus	wheels
carro	*avión*	*autobús*	*ruedas*
boat	ship	hot air balloon	submarine
barco	*crucero*	*globo (aerostático)*	*submarino*
bicycle	train	motorcycle	helicopter
bicicleta	*tren*	*motocicleta*	*helicóptero*
sailboat	truck	rocket	canoe
velero	*camión*	*cohete*	*canoa*

www.bilinguistics.com

Articulation Station

Use these words during any of the structured activities or in homework assignments to target a child's goals.

B

TRANSPORTATION

English

M **m**otorcycle, sub**m**arine, hel**m**et

P helico**p**ter, trans**p**ortation, shi**p**

B **b**us, **b**oat, **b**icycle, hot air **b**alloon, sail**b**oat

K **c**anoe, **c**ar, ro**ck**et, bi**c**ycle, motor**c**ycle, heli**c**opter, tru**ck**

G **g**o, **g**round, **g**arbage truck

T **t**rain, **t**ruck, **t**ranspor**t**ation, mo**t**orcycle, ho**t** air balloon, helicop**t**er, sailboa**t**, boa**t**, rocke**t**, helme**t**, floa**t**, fast

D **d**oor, **d**rive, win**d**ow

F **f**ly, **f**loat, **f**ast, **f**erry

S **s**ubmarine, **s**ailboat, bi**c**ycle, motor**c**ycle, tran**s**portation, fa**st**, bu**s**, wheel**s**

L f**l**y, f**l**oat, he**l**icopter, whee**l**s, hot air ba**ll**oon, sai**l**boat, he**l**ment, bicyc**l**e, motorcyc**l**e

R **r**ocket, **t**rain, t**r**uck, d**r**ive, t**r**anspo**r**tation, ai**r**plane, moto**r**cycle, subma**r**ine, hot ai**r** balloon, ca**r**, helicopte**r**, doo**r**

Curriculum-Based Speech Therapy Activities

Articulation Station

B

TRANSPORTATION

Use these words during any of the structured activities or in homework assignments to target a child's goals.

Spanish

M   **m**otocicleta, sub**m**arino, ca**m**ión

P   **p**uerta, helicó**p**tero, trans**p**ortación

B   **b**ote, **b**arco, **b**icicleta, auto**b**ús, glo**b**o

K   **c**anoa, **c**arro, **c**amión, **c**ohete, **c**asco, **c**arguero, bar**c**o, bi**c**icleta, moto**c**icleta, heli**c**óptero

G   **g**lobo, car**g**uero, va**g**ón

T   **t**ren, **t**ransportación, bo**t**e, mo**t**ocicleta, au**t**obús, ven**t**ana, bicicle**t**a, motocicle**t**a, helicóp**t**ero, cohe**t**e, puer**t**a

D   rue**d**as, rápi**d**o, con**d**ucir

F   **f**erroviario, **f**abricante de canoas, **f**erry

S   **s**ubmarino, bi**c**icleta, moto**c**icleta, ca**s**co, tran**s**portación, autobú**s**, rueda**s**

L   g**l**obo, ve**l**ero, he**l**icóptero, bicic**l**eta, motocic**l**eta

R   **r**uedas, t**r**en, t**r**anspo**r**tación, ba**r**co, submarino, ve**l**ero, ca**rr**o, helicópte**r**o, pue**r**ta, ca**r**gue**r**o, fe**rr**oviario

www.bilinguistics.com

 # Phonology:
Syllable Strips in English

TRANSPORTATION

car ○

boat ○

ship

bus

wheels ○

airplane

rocket

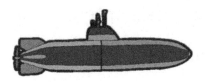
submarine

bicycle

hot air balloon

motorcycle

helicopter

Curriculum-Based Speech Therapy Activities

Phonology:
Syllable Strips in Spanish

TRANSPORTATION

tren

○

avión

○ ○

ruedas

○ ○

camión

○ ○

barco

○ ○

globo

○ ○

autobús

○ ○ ○

velero

○ ○ ○

cohete

○ ○ ○

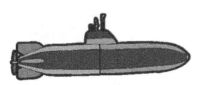

submarino

○ ○ ○ ○

bicicleta

○ ○ ○ ○

motocicleta

○ ○ ○ ○ ○

www.bilinguistics.com

Mini Book:

Color, cut, and create a *WHERE* book about yourself.

D

TRANSPORTATION

Where do we travel?

¿Dónde viajamos?

 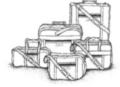

Cars drive on a road.

Los carros manejan a la calle.

Boats float on a river.

Airplanes fly in the sky.

Los barcos flotan en el río.

Los aviones vuelan en el cielo.

Mini Book:

Color, cut, and create a book about people who travel.

E

TRANSPORTATION

Who travels?

¿Quién viaja?

A cowboy rides a horse.

Un vaquero monta un caballo.

A pilot flies a plane.

Un piloto vuela un avión.

A cyclist rides a bicycle.

Un ciclista monta una bicicleta.

www.bilinguistics.com

Table Activity:

Which vehicles are biggest and smallest?

F
TRANSPORTATION

Circle the vehicle that is the biggest. Draw a square around the vehicle that is the smallest.

 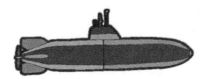 

Curriculum-Based Speech Therapy Activities

Table Activity:

Which vehicle travels on land?

Circle the vehicle that travels on land.

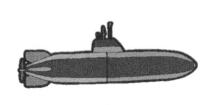  

G **TRANSPORTATION**

Craft:
Train Construction:
Visuospatial shape learning activity

TRANSPORTATION

Cut, color, and connect these pieces into a train.

Materials: scissors, markers, construction paper

# Craft:
Train Construction

TRANSPORTATION

www.bilinguistics.com

Craft:
Sea and Sky

TRANSPORTATION

Paint or color these images as a fun way to follow directions. Talk about shapes and produce prepositional phrases identifying whether something is *in the sea* or *in the sky*.

Materials: paper, different colors or washable paint for finger painting

Recipe:
Traffic Light Recipe

TRANSPORTATION

Demonstrate a traffic light made out of food to increase your students' interest. Then use the activity to take turns, identify colors, follow directions, and sequence.

Materials: graham cracker, peanut butter, red, yellow, and green apples

I want

Yo quiero

graham cracker / *una galleta graham*

peanut butter / *crema de cacahuate*

green yellow, and red apples / *manzanas verdes, amarillas, y rojas*

www.bilinguistics.com

Recipe:
Traffic Light Sequencing

TRANSPORTATION

Use the activity to take turns, identify colors, follow directions, and sequence.

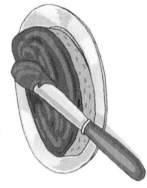

Put peanut butter on a graham cracker.

Pon manteca de cacahuate en una galleta graham.

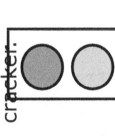

Put the apples on the graham cracker.

Pon las manzanas en la galleta graham.

Get a graham cracker.

Agarra una galleta graham.

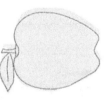

Cut upeeled red, yellow, and green apples.

Corta manzanas rojas, amarillas, y verdes sin pelar.

# Game:

File Folder Game: Transportation  **TRANSPORTATION**

Cut out and paste pictures on the inside of a file folder. Use Velcro or putty to stick a mode of transportation (car, hot air balloon, etc.) from the grab bag activity to the correct home (sky, land or water).

Note: Pictures will cover one and a half pages of the inside of the file folder. Use the extra room on the half page to mount the types of transportation on Velcro or tape a baggie to keep them inside.

Materials: two file folders, glue and Velcro or a sandwich bag

 # Game:

File Folder Game: Transportation

TRANSPORTATION

Curriculum-Based Speech Therapy Activities

Parent Note:
Transportation Coloring

TRANSPORTATION

Hi Parents!

This week we are talking about transportation. Ask your child to share what he knows about transportation you can use on the road, in the water, or in the air.

¡Hola Padres!

Esta semana estamos hablando de la transportación. Platiquen con su hijo sobre el transporte que se puede tomar en el aire, en el agua, o en la tierra.

www.bilinguistics.com

Insects
Los insectos

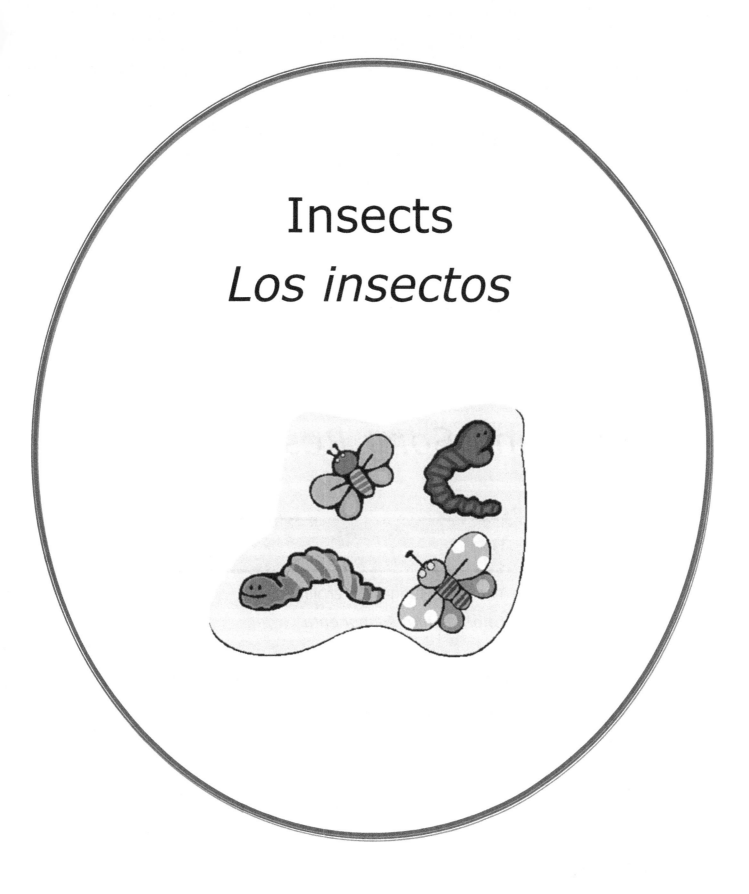

Insects/ los insectos

SONGS

English	Spanish
Ladybug Ladybug	*La cucaracha*
The Ants Go Marching One by One	*Las hormigas van marchando*
I'm Bringing Home a Baby Bumblebee	*Caracol col col*
Itsy Bitsy Spider	*La araña pequeñita*

Songs can be found at http://bilinguistics.com/music-for-speech-therapy/.

Book and Song Resources

BOOK LOCATOR

NON-FICTION

595 Insects and Spiders

Title	Author
The Very Hungry Caterpillar / *La oruga muy hambrienta*	E. Carle
The Grouchy Ladybug	E. Carle
Insect Picnic / *El picnic de los insectos*	A. Rockwell
I'm a Caterpillar / *Soy una oruga*	J. Marzollo
Good Night, Sweet Butterflies	D. Bentley
The Fleas / *Las pulgas*	A. Tison

Insects Unit Content

Section	Schedule	Activity	Goals
A	Surprise Bag	Cut out insect picture cards Other options: • Plastic toy insects • Insect puppets	• Following directions • Utterance expansion • Answering questions • Turn taking
B	Articulation Station	Insect-related words organized by sound for articulation targets Record sounds for examples of correct productions	• Production of correct sounds in words and phrases
C	Phonology Syllable Strips	Insect picture cards in English and Spanish for 1– to 5-syllable words	• Syllable segmentation
D	Mini Book #1	The Parts of an Insect *Las partes de un insecto*	• Verb conjugation • Part-whole relationships • Utterance expansion
E	Mini Book #2	How Do Insects Move? *¿Cómo se mueven los insectos?*	• Spatial concepts • Action words • Utterance expansion
F	Table Activity #1	Semantic Relationships	• Insects and locations • Answering questions • Utterance expansion

www.bilinguistics.com

Insects Unit Content

Section	Schedule	Activity	Goals
G	Table Activity #2	Who's the Smallest One of All?	• Size concepts • Describing • Labeling
H	Craft #1	Make a Ladybug	• Following directions • Labeling insect parts • Requesting materials
I	Craft #2	Egg Carton Ladybug	• Following directions • Basic concepts: part-whole, top/bottom, colors, number • Plurals (leg vs. legs)
J	Recipe	Worms in Dirt	• Following directions • Requesting • Sequencing • Utterance expansion
K	Game	File Folder Game: Let's Catch Bugs!	• Describing actions • Counting • Answering questions • Utterance expansion
L	Parent Note	Insect Coloring Page	• Demonstrate learning • Give parents visual cues to understand and converse with their child

Surprise Bag: Insect Picture Cards

INSECTS

fly	ant	bee	wasp
mosca	*hormiga*	*abeja*	*avispa*
butterfly	beetle	cockroach	ant hill
mariposa	escarabajo	*cucaracha*	hormiguero
caterpillar	wings	antenna	legs
oruga	*alas*	*antena*	*patas*
ladybug	squash	flying	crawling
mariquita	aplastar	*volar*	*arrastrarse*

www.bilinguistics.com

Articulation Station

Use these words during any of the structured activities or in homework assignments to target a child's goals.

B

INSECTS

English

M   **m**oth, **m**osquito, wor**m**

P   grasho**pp**er, cater**p**illar

B   **b**ug, **b**ee, **b**ody, **b**ite, **b**eetle, **b**utterfly

K   **c**o**c**oon, **ch**rysalis, **c**aterpillar, **c**o**ck**roach, **c**ri**ck**et, mos**qu**ito

G   **g**arden, bu**g**, dra**g**onfly, win**g**, e**gg**

T   an**t**enna, bi**t**e, ne**t**, ea**t**, an**t**, mosqui**t**o, insec**t**

D   **d**irt, la**d**ybug, hea**d**

F   **f**irefly, **f**ly, **f**lower, lea**f**

S   gra**ss**, gra**ss**hopper

L   **l**eg, **l**eaf, **l**adybug, beet**l**e, f**l**y, f**l**ower

R   wo**r**m, c**r**icket, g**r**asshoppe**r**, cock**r**oach

Articulation Station

Use these words during any of the structured activities or in homework assignments to target a child's goals.

INSECTS

Spanish

M   **m**osca, **m**ariposa, **m**ariquita, hor**m**iga

P   **p**atas, **p**icar, **p**ulga, mari**p**osa

B   **b**icho, **v**olar, a**b**eja, hue**v**o

K   **c**ome, **c**abeza, **c**olmena, **c**u**c**aracha, pi**c**ar, mari**qu**ita, mo**sc**a

G   **g**usano, **g**rillo, oru**g**a, hormi**g**a

T   **t**ierra, pa**t**as, mariqui**t**a, *insec**t**o

D   jar**d**ín, re**d**

F   **f**lor

S   **s**alta, **s**altamonte**s**, **c**iempié**s**, gu**s**ano, maripo**s**a, pata**s**

L   **l**ombriz, a**l**a, vo**l**ar, vue**l**e

R   g**r**illo, o**r**uga, cuca**r**acha, ma**r**iquita, lomb**r**iz, tie**rr**a

www.bilinguistics.com

Phonology:
Syllable Strips in English

INSECTS

bee
○

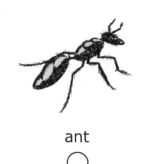
ant
○

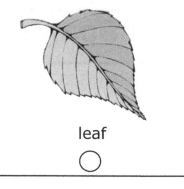
leaf
○

honey
○ ○

beetle
○ ○

flower
○ ○

butterfly
○ ○ ○

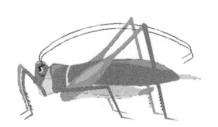
grasshopper
○ ○ ○

mosquito
○ ○ ○

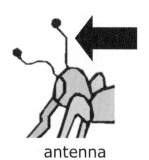
antenna
○ ○ ○

caterpillar
○ ○ ○ ○

praying mantis
○ ○ ○ ○

144   Curriculum-Based Speech Therapy Activities

Phonology:
Syllable Strips in Spanish

INSECTS

miel
○

flor
○

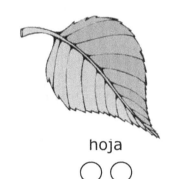
hoja
○ ○

mosca
○ ○

abeja
○ ○ ○

hormiga
○ ○ ○

zancudo
○ ○ ○

colmena
○ ○ ○

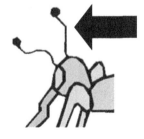
antena
○ ○ ○

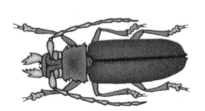
cucaracha
○ ○ ○ ○

escarabajo
○ ○ ○ ○ ○

saltamontes
○ ○ ○ ○

www.bilinguistics.com

Mini Book:

Cut, color, and create a book about insect parts.

INSECTS — D

The Parts of an Insect

Las partes de un insecto

Every insect has a head.

Cada insecto tiene una cabeza.

Every insect has a thorax.

Cada insecto tiene un tórax.

Every insect has an abdomen.

Cada insecto tiene un abdomen.

Mini Book:

Cut, color, and create a book about how insects move.

E

INSECTS

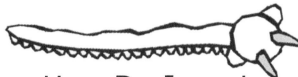

How Do Insects Move?

¿Cómo se mueven los insectos?

Bees fly high in the sky!

¡Las abejas vuelan alto en el cielo!

Spiders crawl on their web!

¡Las arañas se arrastran en su web!

Crickets hop all around!

¡Los grillos saltan por todos lados!

Table Activity:
Semantic Relationships

INSECTS

Draw a line between the two pictures that go together.
Color if time permits.

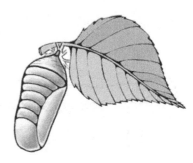

Curriculum-Based Speech Therapy Activities

Table Activity:
Who's the smallest one of all?

Circle the smallest insect in each line.

INSECTS

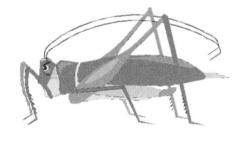  

 # Craft: Make a Ladybug

INSECTS

Suggested book: *The Grouchy Ladybug/La mariquita malhumorada*

Materials (per student): ladybug mat, red construction paper (2 semicircles), black construction paper (4 spots), brass fasteners (2)

Directions for Adult:

1. Print and cut the ladybug mat (see opposite page) for each child.
2. Using patterns, cut 2 red semicircles and 4 small black circles from construction paper. (Tip: Fold construction paper multiple times so you get several circles per cut.)
3. Line up ladybug wings on body and pre-pierce holes through the gray dots on the ladybug's wings and body.

Directions for Student:

1. Pick a ladybug mat.
2. Select two red semicircles (i.e. the wings) and attach to the ladybug body. Put fasteners through the holes in the wings and body.
3. Glue the black spots to the red wings.
4. Open and close the wings to help the ladybug fly!

Instrucciones para el estudiante:

1. Escoge tu alfombrilla de mariquita.
2. Elije dos semicírculos rojos (las alas) y sujétalas al cuerpo de la mariquita. Pon los broches latonados por las alas y por el cuerpo.
3. Pega las manchas negras en las alas rojas.
4. ¡Abre y cierra las alas para ayudar a tu mariquita a volar!

Craft: Make a Ladybug

INSECTS

Ladybug Mat:

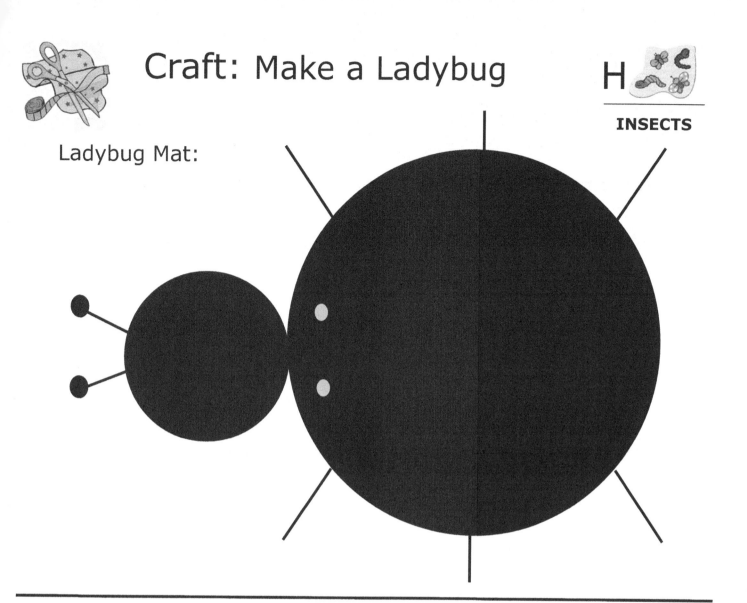

Patterns:

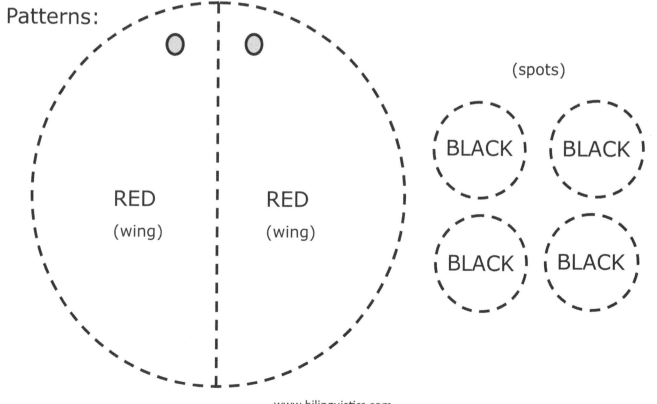

RED (wing)   RED (wing)

(spots)

BLACK   BLACK

BLACK   BLACK

www.bilinguistics.com

Craft:
Lady Bug Egg Carton

INSECTS

Suggested book: *The Grouchy Ladybug/La mariquita malhumorada*

Materials needed: red and black paint, single cups cut from egg cartons or paper cups, paintbrushes, googly eyes, glue, pipe cleaners

Directions for Adult:

This is a great activity to introduce long term projects. Each step is simple and short and the student s get excited each time they get to come back and work on their ladybug again.

1. Cut egg cartons into individual cups. There should be 12 cups from one full size carton. You will need 1 cup per ladybug.
2. Cut pipe cleaners into 2-inch pieces. You will need 6 pieces for ladybug legs and 2 pieces for the antennas.
3. Pierce holes in carton cup for legs and antennas.

Directions for Student:

1. Paint the cup red.
2. Paint black dots.
3. Glue on the eyes.
4. Put each foot into the holes on the bottom.
5. Put each antenna into the hole on top.

Instrucciones para el estudiante:

1. Pinta la taza roja.
2. Pinta las manchas negras.
3. Pega los ojos.
4. Pon cada pata por los agujeros en la parte abajo.
5. Pon cada antena por los agujeros en la parte arriba.

Recipe:
Worms in Dirt

INSECTS

Tell students that today you are going to eat dirt and worms! ...but that it's not real dirt! Use the activity to practice making requests, following directions, taking turns, and describing.

*Note: Be sure to check with parents about allergies and dietary restrictions.

Materials: large bowl, mixing spoon, cups, spoons, chocolate pudding mix, milk, crushed chocolate sandwich cookies, gummy worms

I want

Yo quiero

a cup

una taza

cookie crumbs

migas de galleta

worm

un gusano

www.bilinguistics.com

Recipe:
Worms in Dirt

INSECTS

Demonstrate learning or pre-teach the activity with a sequencing activity.

Scoop pudding into cup.

Echa el pudín en la taza.

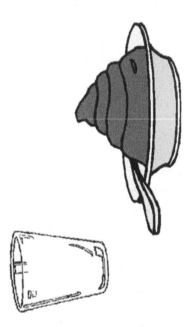

Put worms in the dirt!

¡Pon los gusanos en la tierra!

Stir milk and pudding mix.

Revuelva la leche y el pudín.

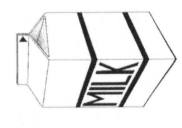

Put cookie crumbs on top of the pudding.

Pon las migas encima del pudín.

Game:
Let's catch bugs

INSECTS

Preparation: Print page with bug jar and attach to the inside of a file folder. Attach Velcro pieces to the picture scene (8 pieces in the sky and 8 pieces inside the jar). Print page with bugs and die onto cardstock; color if desired. Cut out die template and assemble. Cut out bugs, laminate, and attach Velcro to the back.

To play: First child rolls die and follows directions. The child can collect 1-3 bugs or roll again. If one bug flies away, the child must remove a bug from the jar to return to the sky. If the jar tips, all bugs escape from the jar and play starts again!

Materials: file folder, glue, cardstock, (crayons/markers), and Velcro

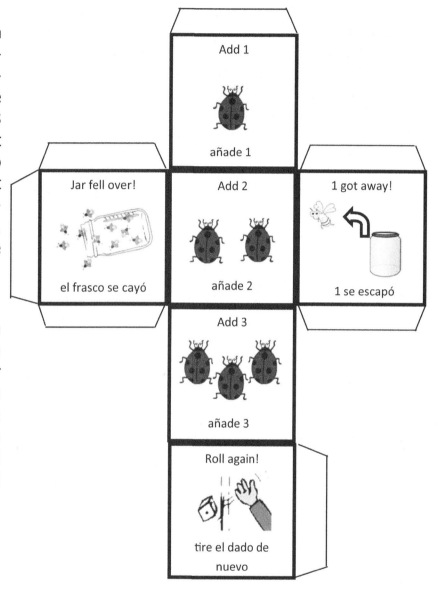

www.bilinguistics.com

Game:
Let's Catch Bugs!

INSECTS

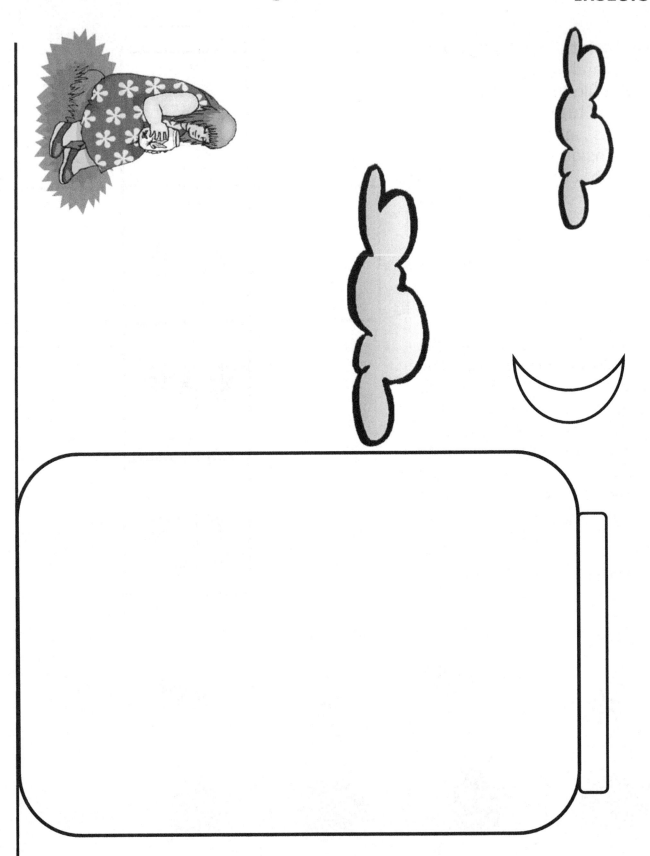

Parent Note:
Insect Coloring Page

INSECTS

Hi Parents!

This week we are talking about insects. Ask your child to share what he knows about the insects below.

Hola Padres!

Esta semana hablamos de los insectos. Platiquen con su hijo/a sobre lo que sabe de los insectos abajo.

www.bilinguistics.com

REFERENCES

Beckwith, L. & Cohen, S.E. (1989). Maternal responsiveness with preterm infants and later competency. In M.H. Bornstein (Ed.). *Maternal responsiveness: Characteristics and consequences: New directions for child development* (pp. 75-87). San Francisco: Jossey Bass.

Dempsey, I., & Dunst, C.J. (2004). Help-giving styles as a function of parent empowerment in families with a young child with a disability. *Journal of Intellectual and Developmental Disability, 29*, 50-61.

Frey, K. S., Fewell, R. R., & Vadasy, P. F. (1989). The relationship between changes in parental adjustment and child outcome in families of young handicapped children. *Topics in Early Childhood Special Education, 8*, (4), 38-57.

Krauss, M.W. (1993). Child-related and parenting stress: Similarities and differences between mothers and fathers of children with disabilities. *American Journal on Mental Retardation, 97,* (4), 393-404.

Rogoff, B. (1990). *Apprenticeship in Thinking.* Oxford: Oxford University Press.

Rosetti, L. (2006). *The Rosetti Infant-Toddler Language Scale*. East Moline, IL: LinguiSystems, Inc.

Tomasello, M., & Farrar, MJ. (1986). Joint attention and early language. *Child Development, 57,* (6), 1454-1463.

Vygotsky, L.S. (1967). Play and its role in the mental development of the child. *Soviet Psychology, 5*, 6-18.

Made in United States
North Haven, CT
24 August 2024

56494668R00089